Our Black Seminarians and Black Clergy without A Black Theology

Our Black Seminarians and Black Clergy without A Black Theology:
The Tragedy of Black People/Africans in Religion Today

By
Yosef A.A. ben-Jochannan

Our Black Seminarians and Black Clergy without A Black Theology

ISBN 0-933121-62-8
LCCC Number 96-84728

Founded in 1978, Black Classic Press specializes in bringing to light obscure and significant works by and about people of African descent. If our books are not available in your area, ask your local bookseller to order them. Our current list of titles can be obtained by writing:

Black Classic Press
c/o List
P.O. Box 13414
Baltimore, MD 21203

Visit our website www.blackclassic.com
A Young Press With Some Very Old Ideas

Our Black Seminarians
An Introduction
by
John Henrik Clarke

Like a well-structured house, the extensive writings of Yosef ben Jochannan rest figuratively on four strong pillars. Those pillars include *Black Man of the Nile and His Family*, *Africa: Mother of Western Civilization*, *African Origins of the Major "Western Religions,"* and the fourth pillar, *Black Seminarians and Black Clergy without a Black Theology*. Considering the times that we live in and the assault on the African mind by conquerors, the fourth pillar might be the most important. The greatest destruction of Europeans and Arabs in Africa was not the physical conquest of the continent and its people, their greatest feats were the conquest of the African mind, the tragic destruction of African institutions, and their denigration of African civilization as "primitive."

That Europeans mocked and ridiculed African traditional belief systems was deplorable, but the real tragedy is that most of European-trained Africans did likewise. Influenced by the European propaganda mills, some Africans began to believe that they had produced nothing of worth. Edward Wilmot Blyden, the nineteenth century Caribbean activist, observed that Africans believed that their only chance of rising to a position of respectful manhood and womanhood was to strive to be most unlike themselves. This is the origin of Black seminarians without a Black theology.

Europeans not only enslaved the African's body, they crippled and enslaved the African's hope, his aspirations, and to a great extent his imagination. This crime is unique in history because it has never happened quite the same way to another people. The reverberations of this crime are still with us because we are delinquent in understanding the role the three major world religions played in setting the crime in motion and in rationalizing the propaganda used for the continuation of the crime. We need to look back in order to look forward. We need to address a painful issue for ourselves and for our children. What role did organized religion play in creating this crime in the first place and what role does it play in sustaining this crime?

The ideas, the practices, and the concepts that went into the making of Judaism, Christianity, and Islam were already old in Africa before Europe was born. African people have a great strength and a great weakness. Their great strength is their ability to be open-minded, humane, and hospitable to strangers. Their great weakness, political and otherwise, is that they have never become astute at examining the intentions of strangers who enter their homes. To this day, Africans find it hard to believe that anyone would come into Africa to do African people harm.

The enemies of Africa have always thought of Africa as a prize, because from earliest times, Africa was and still is the world's richest continent. If Africa is indeed the world's richest continent, but is full of impoverished people, then something has gone wrong with the management of the resources of this continent. There is not one country in Africa where the Africans are the sole manager of the wealth generating resources of their respective countries. A greater tragedy is that not a single country in Africa today bases its law and religion on the traditional culture and religions of the African people. Every state in Africa is an imitation of a European state. In form, these states are alien to the original design of African states, which were multiethnic territorial states with loose borders, when they had borders at all. The African-organized states permitted a cross fertilization of people, cultures, and institutions. The nation state imposed on Africa by Europeans is a political straight-jacket retarding African development. This artificial state divides African cultures between national borders and prevents consolidations that formerly led to African multiethnic empires.

In the old African states, many belief systems were practiced within the state without conflict. Many states practiced and lived by values that would later be called *Christianity*. This was thousands of years before Christ was born. They governed themselves by concepts that would later be called *socialism* not only before Karl Marx was born but before Europe was born. The invaders of Africa extracted certain practices as well as spiritual and philosophical thought from Africa, formalized and dogmatized them, and then sold them back to the Africans as something new. To this day Africans have not realized that their own indigenous belief systems were better suited to them than any religion imposed on them by the foreigners, fakers, and fools who came into Africa. The proselytizers and followers of Christianity and Islam in Africa declared war on every form of African culture that did not suit their political purpose.

The Arab was an invader and a conqueror in Egypt and subsequently in other parts of Africa. In most cases in history, the invader and the conqueror came to rule, and to exploit, not to civilize. What passes for civilization in recently conquered countries is the imposition of control and rules of conduct by the conqueror to facilitate his domination of native people. The light of indigenous civilization is often extinguished in the process. As invaders and conquerors in Egypt and in Africa, Arabs were no different from other conquerors in world history. The Arab conquest of Egypt occurred at a time when North Africans, like Native Americans, mistakenly called *Indians*, became a victim of their own charity. They looked with favor on a conqueror that they thought would be a friend.

Because Europeans of the Hebrew faith and people of the Hebrew faith in general have sent no missionaries of any significance to Africa, it might be assumed that there is nothing to be said about them in relationship to Africa. This assumption is basically true in matters relating to the large and scattered number of people of the Hebrew faith that live outside of Europe. European Jews, however, have behaved no different from other Europeans to African people. They played a role in the rise of the European slave trade, and they played a role in European colonialism in Africa and of the broader world. They often played a role in colonizing other people of the Hebrew faith who were not of European extraction.

The Hebrew faith is international and is not a monopoly of Europeans who practice the faith. Europe is the historical homeland of the European Jew. At this point we must make a clear distinction between the Western Asian people of ancient times and present-day Europeans who are belated converts to the Hebrew faith. When European Jews claim Palestine as their ancient homeland, they are claiming an area that existed before Europe existed. If any legitimate claim can be made for Palestine at all it should be made by the descendants of the Hebrew faith from Western Asia not by the contemporary European Jews. The European Jews' claim on Palestine is shrouded in Biblical myth and may not be supportable by historical evidence because there has been no religious partnership between Europeans of the Hebrew faith and the vast number of non-Europeans of that faith who live outside of Europe.

In discussing the influence of members of the Hebrew faith on Africa, I am dealing mainly with Europeans. Their influence on Africa has been mainly commercial and only marginally cultural. The people of the Hebrew faith, who would later be referred to as Jews, entered world history through a visit to Africa—it was in Africa that they became a people. Their later search for a homeland was motivated by their troubles in Europe with other Europeans who decided not to accept their religious and cultural way of life, although physically most European Jews are indistinguishable from other Europeans.

The notion of Black seminarians without a Black theology is not completely new. The African awareness movement of the nineteenth century was moving in the direction of seeking African solutions to African problems in the Caribbean Islands and in Africa itself. Its greatest spokesman was Edward Wilmot Blyden, especially in his books *Christianity, Islam and the Negro Race* and a smaller work, *African Life and Customs*. In the United States, Prince Hall from Barbados, developed the first black Masonic order and called it The African Lodge. Richard Allen developed the African Methodist

Episcopal Church. The African American community was *Africa-identified* in the names of its churches and institutions without shame or apology. There was an African cultural basis to the successful slave revolts in the Caribbean Islands, Brazil, and in other parts of South America. In 1829, David Walker issued his famous *Appeal To the Coloured People of the World*, summoning them to take up arms against their oppressors. Haitian revolutions set revolts in motion in the United States, the Caribbean Islands, and in South America. Two of the initial leaders of the Haitian Revolution were African priests preaching African cultural awareness in an African language. The first half of the nineteenth century saw the rise of Back-to-Africa movements, Negro Convention movements, and "Resettlement" movements, mainly focused on Africa, especially Liberia. Martin Delany and the Jamaican Robert Campbell went to Africa to search for a place of settlement. In the period before the Civil War, African fever had created a new intellectual environment among the so-called free Negroes both in the United States and in the Caribbean Islands. Many of those who could not go back to Africa physically were trying to go back psychologically.

Near the end of the nineteenth century, Bishop Turner emerged preaching new and dynamic sermons about Africa and why we should return and claim it. He began his dynamic preaching about the time Marcus Garvey was born, and his activities went on well into the twentieth century. His book *Respect Black* contains his best speeches. Robert Redkey has written an outstanding account of Bishop Turner in *Black Exodus*. These writings were the stimulus that lead us to a consideration of Marcus Garvey, Malcolm X and Elijah Muhammed.

While I agree with ben Jochannan that today we have Black seminarians without a Black theology, there is a need to look at some of our religious and political activists who were seriously aware of this defect and tried to do something about it. In Africa, we need to study the works of Joseph B. Danquah, especially his book *The Akan Doctrine of God*, and Kofee Asara's *West African Religions*. The writings of John S. Mbiti are informative in spite of the fact that he is an African Christian writing about African traditional beliefs.

In its traditions, ceremonies, and practices, the Baptist Church in the United States is the most African in spite of the fact that most Baptists are unaware of it. Reverend Albert B. Cleage, Jr., (Jaramogi Abebe Agyeman), has done the most in recent years to take the Black church back to its African base and to change the color and emphasis of the deity referred to as Jesus Christ. He opens his book *The Black Messiah* with the following words:

> For nearly five hundred years the illusion that Jesus was white dominated the world only because white Europeans dominated the world. Now, with the emergence of the nationalist movements of the world's colored majority, the historic truth is finally beginning to emerge—that Jesus was the nonwhite leader of a nonwhite people struggling for national liberation against the rule of a white nation, Rome. The intermingling of the races in Africa and the Mediterranean area is an established fact. The Nation Israel was a mixture of Chaldeans, Egyptians, Midianites, Ethiopians, Kushites, Babylonians and other dark peoples, all of whom were already mixed with the black people of Central Africa. That white Americans continue to insist upon a white Christ in the face of all historical evidence to the contrary and despite the hundreds of shrines to Black Madonnas all over the world, is the crowning demonstration of their white supremacist conviction that all things good and valuable must be white. On the other hand, until black Christians are ready to challenge this lie, they have not freed themselves from their spiritual bondage to the white man nor established in their own minds their right to first-class citizenship in Christ's kingdom on earth. Black people cannot build dignity on their knees worshipping a white Christ. We must put down this white Jesus which the white man gave us in slavery and which has been tearing us to pieces.

In another book, *Black Christian Nationalism*, Reverend Cleage in his creed declares:

> I believe that human society stands under the judgement of one God, revealed to all, and known by many names. His creative power is visible in the mysteries of the universe, in the revolutionary Holy Spirit which will not long permit men to endure injustice nor to wear the shackles of bondage, in the rage of the powerless when they

struggle to be free, and in the violence and conflict which even now threaten to level the hills and the mountains.

I believe that Jesus, the Black Messiah, was a revolutionary leader, sent by God to rebuild the Black Nation Israel and to liberate Black people from powerlessness and from the oppression, brutality, and exploitation of the white gentile world.

I believe that the revolutionary spirit of God, embodied in the Black Messiah, is born anew in each generation and that Black Christian Nationalists constitute the living remnant of God's Chosen People in this day, and are charged by Him with responsibility for the Liberation of Black people.

I believe that both my survival and my salvation depend upon my willingness to reject INDIVIDUALISM and so I commit my life to the Liberation Struggle of Black people and accept the values, ethics, morals, and program of the Black Nation defined by that struggle, and taught by the Black Christian Nationalist Movement.

If a line is forming behind this kind of perspective, I would like to be at the head of the line or at least close to it. When we consider the literature that was produced in Africa, the Caribbean Islands, and in the United States in the nineteenth century and its continuation into the twentieth century it is evident that our direction was positive. Although there are Black seminarians and Black clergy without a Black theology as ben Jochannan has asserted, this issue did not totally escape all of our thinkers and freedom fighters trying to deliver us from the bondage of our oppressor. We need commitment and sincerity in this fight to reclaim our spiritual being, which is the essence of our humanity. When African people throughout the world produce a sizeable group of teachers, thinkers, and intellectuals dedicated to a theology of liberation, they will in turn bring into being a revolution that will change the world and create a new humanity for African people and the rest of the world. The long night of our oppression and our love/hate romance with our oppressor will be over, and then we can walk out into the sunlight of a new day.

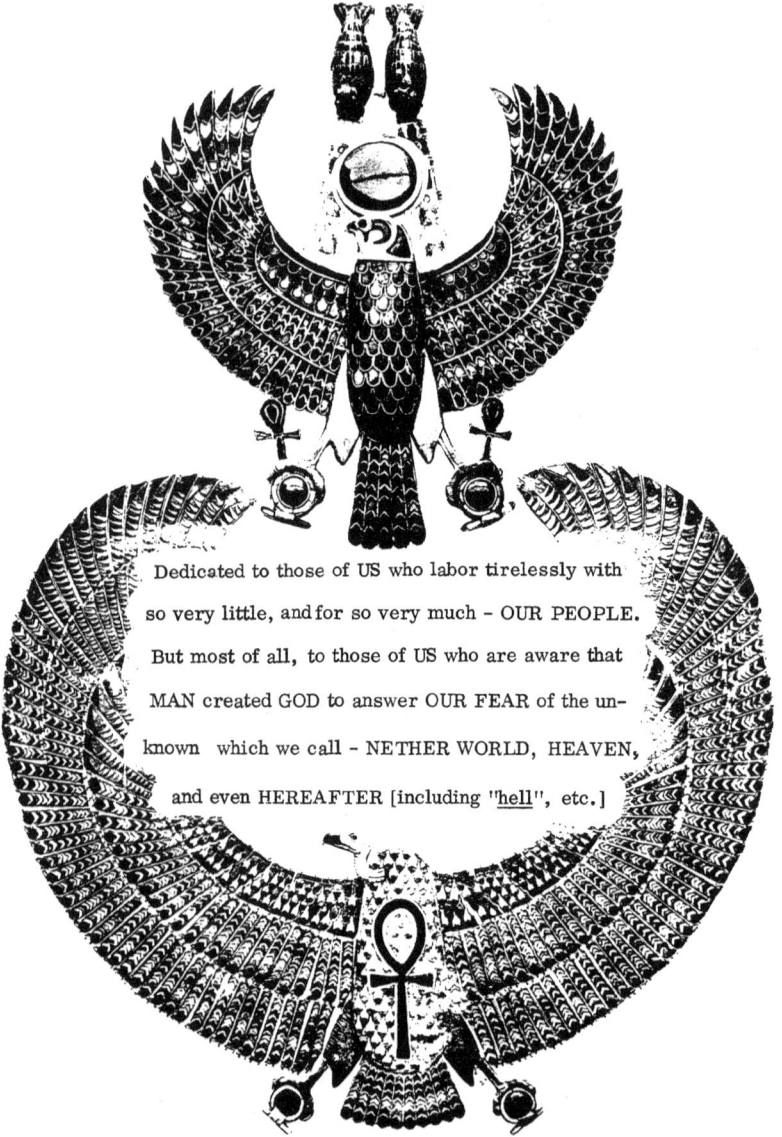

Dedicated to those of US who labor tirelessly with
so very little, and for so very much - OUR PEOPLE.
But most of all, to those of US who are aware that
MAN created GOD to answer OUR FEAR of the unknown which we call - NETHER WORLD, HEAVEN,
and even HEREAFTER [including "hell", etc.]

AFRICAN/BLACK SPIRITUALS
FROM A "BLACK THEOLOGY" OF YESTERDAY:

Oh Freedom! Oh Freedom!
Oh Freedom I love Thee!
And before I'll be a slave,
I'll be buried in my grave,
And go home to my Lord and be free

XXXXXX

Go tell it on de Mountain
Three Wise Men to Jerusalem came
Lit'l Boy, how ole are you?
Dar's Star in de East
Mary had a Baby
Rise up Shepherd an' foller

XXXXXX

Swing low chariot! Pray let me in!
For I don't want to stay behind.
Swing low chariot! Pray just let me in!
For I don't want to stay here no longer.

XXXXXX

The three AFRICAN [so-called "Negro"] SPIRITUALS above have been suppressed by too many so-called "MINISTERS OF THE GOSPEL OF JESUS CHRIST, CHOIRMASTERS, MUSICAL DIRECTORS", et al in preference for their White masters' [so-called] "CLASSICAL MUSIC" each and every Sunday; thus Handel's "MESSIAH" and other German, Welch, Dutch, English, Scottish, French, Italian, etc. European and European-American LILY WHITE RACIST SONGS. The most tradgic of all being the following:
"MAKE ME WHITER THAN SNOW O'LORD".[1]
This is the same reason why African/Black People can still feel comfortable in so-called "Christian Organizations" that take their money, and still curse them by reminding them that they are the result of a "CURSE" God placed upon them because of the "NOAH AND THE FLOOD" allegory.

Certainly this volume, particularly its pictorial documentation, should add to the "EDUCATION", not "MISEDUCATION" we are subjected to in the "NEGRO CLERGY" and "NEGRO SEMINARIES" and other "NEGRO INSTITUTIONS", of ourselves. This is only possible if we are willing to read everything we can about the origin of so-called "WESTERN RELIGIONS": JUDAISM, CHRISTIANITY AND ISLAM from their African Nile Valley and Great Lakes base..........Amen-Ra.

1. Wm. G. Fischer, "Whiter Than Snow", Baptist Hymnal, Convention Press, Nashville, Tenn., 1956. p. 201.

A "BLACK THEOLOGIAN":

HE LEARNT, TAUGHT AND PREACHED A "BLACK THEOLOGY"

It is not the length of life that counts;
not how long we live, but how well.

OBSEQUIES

Above and beyond the reach of a "DEDICATION"
this work is published by the author in

HONOURED SACRED MEMORIUM

to

Our Departed Prophetic Leader
JOMO IREGI [J. H.]

The manuscript for this volume was completed before the passing of my dear friend and
adopted brother Jomo Iregi [James Holloman].
Thus in giving my "WORDS OF COMFORT"
during the "ORDER OF SERVICE" I could not
help but remind his family, hundreds of faithful friends and congregation that it was he who
was most instrumental in convincing me of its
current need; advising that I:
 "WRITE A SUBJECTIVE TREATISE ON
  BLACK THEOLOGY FOR YOUNG
  BLACK PEOPLE OF THE
  20th CENTURY C.E. OR
  A.D. AND BEYOND."

THE REVEREND
JAMES HOLLOMAN
1930 - 1975

Saturday, January 25. 1975 - 11:00 AM

United Missionary Baptist Church
18th at Minnesota Street, Middletown, Ohio

AND BELIEVED IN A "BLACK MESSIAH"

The late Jomo Iregi [otherwise known as Reverend James Holloman] taught a "BLACK THE-
OLOGY" that was mindful of the analysis and facts cited by your author from the works of himself
and others. Some of the works I will be citing have been to date unpublished manuscripts, taped
speeches, and artifacts, etc., all of which Jomo Iregi read by virtue of my introduction of them.
But he was never to see any of the vast majority of the information in printed form in my own
works following the latter part of 1974 C.E. Why? Because life suddenly ended for this wonderful
brother. He had arranged his entire life to be in the service of his fellow African/Black People.
Yes; He was "MURDERED", even though the medical report concerning his DEATH concluded
that he died from...

"A MASSIVE CEREBAL HEMORRHAGE"....

The medical verdict was one thing. But what caused it was another. The "truth" is that Jomo Iregi
died because his fellow "BLACK" [in fact "Negro" and/or "Colored" mostly] "CLERGY" persecuted
and prosecuted him, no less so than the Jews and Romans of the days of Joshua Crystos [otherwise
renamed "Jesus the Christ"/Jesus the Annointed, etc.] persecuted and prosecuted him. Even many
who said, and also holleed,..."YES LORD"... from their pew as he broke loose with gems of our
BLACK/AFRICAN THEOLOGY dealing with the "BLACK MESSIAH JESUS", his father JOSEPH
and mother MARY, could not truly accept him fully. Because he could no longer preach the old-
style "NEGRO RELIGION'S" Lily White Theology of "MARY'S IMMACULATE CONCEPTION" and
JESUS' VIRGIN BIRTH", all without the benefit of GODLY SEXUAL INTERCOURSE - the only personal evidence of "CHILD BIRTH" common to mankind. This latter PREGNANCY BY A GHOST,
forced upon the minds of African People by European Bishops from the NICENE CONFERENCE OF
BISHOPS in ca. 325 C.E./A.D. by way of the SLAVE PLANTATION OWNERS in the seventeenth
century of the Common Era until the technical end of SLAVERY in ca. 1863 C.E., and after through
the entire so-called "RECONSTRUCTION PERIOD/ERA", had no different impact than the following
from the Europeanized VERSIONS of the NEW and OLD TESTAMENT that became for years a basis
upon which "NEGRO/COLORED SEMINARIES" and the "NEGRO/COLORED CLERGY" they produce
acted. Thus the following:

"SLAVE OBEY YOUR MASTER";
and,

"RENDER UNTO CAESAR THAT WHICH IS OF CAESAR, AND UNTO THE
LORD THAT WHICH IS OF THE LORD" [meaning Jesus the Christ].

The saddest of all of this is that the same Lily White Racist "CHRISTIAN" and "JEWISH"
Clergy's forerunners had already claimed as their OWN what you will read on the following pages
that relate to the so-called "NEW TESTAMENT" and OLD TESTAMENT", etc. This, Jomo Iregi

was convinced, was due to their need to PLAGIARIZE and DISTORT the African/Black slaves' ancestors religions, gods, goddesses, theosophy, theology, etc., including even the so-called "TEN COMMANDMENTS" from the "ONE HUNDRED AND FORTY-SEVEN NEGATIVE CONFESSIONS" Moses also DISTORTED and PLAGIARIZED in ca. 1196 B.C.E. on Mt. Horeb in the Sinai Desert of Ta-Merry [Egypt], North Africa. These are the same"NEGATIVE CONFESSIONS" anyone can see in the BOOK OF THE COMING FORTH BY DAY AND BY NIGHT [Egyptian Book Of The Dead, as translated from Hieroglyph into English by Sir E.A.W. Budge], and quite a few of which you can read on page 26 and 27 of this volume.

Jomo Iregi tried to teach his fellow "BLACK CLERGYMEN" and "BLACK CLERGYWOMEN" the truth about the ORIGIN OF JUDAISM and JUDAEO-CHRISTIANITY, only to have them forced him out of the town/city of Dayton, Ohio; they having equally tried to do the same in Middletown, Ohio. I am sorry to say that even in his own UNITED BAPTIST CHURCH he could not overcome the already complete BRAINWASHED MINDS of assistants who were too much CONDITIONED into the STOMPING, DANCING, YELLING, TESTIFYING, "HELL AND DAMNATION", DEMONIC type of Judaeo-Christianity taught to the "NEGRO SEMINARIANS" and parroted by the "NEGRO/CO-LORED CLERGY" of which he refused to follow after completing his own training at Payne College.

When he dared to place on the wall of the vestibule of his church an almost life-size painting of a "BLACK MADONNA AND CHILD", which in fact represented any MOTHER and her CHILD no less than MARY and JESUS ["the Christ/Annointed"], many left the church. Many others remained for just a little more time, but equally found the doors to the street much more acceptable than having to see a sister BLACK WOMAN holding her own BLACK CHILD as the WHITE PEOPLE they were already accustomed to call VIRGIN MARY AND CHILD. In LILY WHITE THEOLOGY they were never made to understand that Michaelangelo painted the very first LILY WHITE JESUS "the Christ"[under commission of Pope Julius II during the years ca. 1509 - 1512 C.E./A.D.] on the ceiling of the Cistene Chaple of St Peter's Basilica, Rome, Italy. Worst of all, they do not know that the models this artist used for the "HOLY FAMILY" was in fact his UNCLE as Joseph, UNCLE'S WIFE as Mary, and UNCLE'S SON as Jesus "the Christ". Thus what they look at each time they see their stained-glass window in their respective church is not "JESUS" [the Christ], but in fact MICHAELANGELO'S FIRST COUSIN". Examine church records for further documentation.

Jomo Iregi installed a LIBRARY in the basement of his church. He tried to make each member understand WHY, and for WHAT, he and/or she is a "CHRISTIAN" - follower of the "BLACK MESSIAH JESUS". But this too was a bit more than most could accept; RELIGION WITH REASON! Yes, he preached a "BLACK THEOLOGY" that dealt with INTELLEGENCE; for this he is no longer with us. Why? He had to give too much of himself; even beyond his physical ability...Amen-Ra.

WHAT, OR WHO, MADE THE DEITIES/GODS OF JUDAISM [Ywh/Jehovah], CHRISTIANITY [Jesus the Christ], ISLAM [Al'lah] AND ALL OF THE [so-called] JUDAEO-CHRISTIAN -ISLAMIC RELIGIONS MORE HOLY/SACRED THAN THESE SHOWN BELOW; THE SAME BEING EQUALLY TRUE FOR THE GODESS "MARY" ABOVE THE GODESS "ISIS"/MARY'S ANCESTOR ?

A SCENE FROM THE HERCULANEUM WORSHIP OF ISIS. This form of worship of the first Virgin Mother was common among the ancient Greeks and Romans in Greece and Rome for hundreds of years before, and up to, the adoption of "African Christianity" by the Roman Emperor Constantine "the great" in ca. 312 C.E. upon his rise to the throne. [From a fresco dating back to the pre-Christian Era in Rome]

Gilbert Schneider
The "Afo-A-Kom" in a photograph taken with special permission before it disappeared.

EVERYWHERE THERE IS A GOD OF GODS

[Left] A scene from the BOOK OF THE DEAD. Osiris - "LORD OF THE DEAD" - looks in the direction of God - HORUS - leading Ani, who has gained "IMMORTALITY" after His Death.

[Right] Another of the major GODS of the universe, who is as "IMMORTAL" to His believers as others believe in their "GOD" or GODS. Quetzalcoatl - the AZTEC MESSIAH - of the entire world.

The Mexican Messiah Quetzalcoatl

Answer

THOSE WHO CREATED THE RELIGIOUS INSTITUTIONS OF THE JEWS, CHRISTIANS AND MUSLIMS/MOSLEMS, ET AL, ALONG WITH THEIR "HOLY SCRIBES, PROPHETS, SAINTS, GODS, DEVILS, DEMONS, ETC.

ALL OF THE DEITIES/GODS AND GODESSES SYMBOLIZED ABOVE PRECEDED THE GODS AND GODESSES...YWH, JESUS, AL'LAH AND MARY...OF JUDAISM, CHRISTIANITY AND ISLAM....Amen-Ra.

PICTORIAL SCENES OF CREATION AND HEAVEN IN HISTORY
[see page xiv]

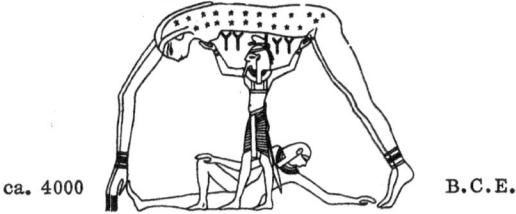

ca. 4000   B.C.E.

SHU - the Air God - holding NUT the
Sky Goddess from the embrace of GEB
- the Earth God lying on the horizontal.
The stars on NUT indicate her celestial nature; the Y shape symbols
indicate the Four Supports of Heaven and Evolution [Procreation].

Section of an early Christian
concept of the Creation Of Eve
out of Adam, and the Serpent Of
Eden.[From a sarcophagus in the
Lateran Museum, Rome, Italy]

ca. 3692 B.C.E.

ca. 4000   B.C.E.

Ptah, an Egyptian creator-god [from a
statue in the Manchester Museum]

Adam and Eve picking the
Forbidden Fruit [From a
painting on the ceiling of the
Cisteen Chapel, Rome].

ca. 3692 B.C.E.

ca. 4000   B.C.E.

CHNUM - the God Of Creation - fashions
the First People on His Potter's Wheel.
[Egyptian conception of The Creation from a bas-relief depicting the birth
of Pharaoh Amenhotep - father of Akhenaten - at Luxor or Thebes, Egypt]

WHEN SEXUAL INTERCOURSE WAS ONE/UNITY WITH GOD

The Worship Of Woman "Before The Fall Of Eve In The Garden Of Eden" Somewhere In Asia

WOMAN AS "HEAVEN" BEFORE "ADAM AND EVE" WERE

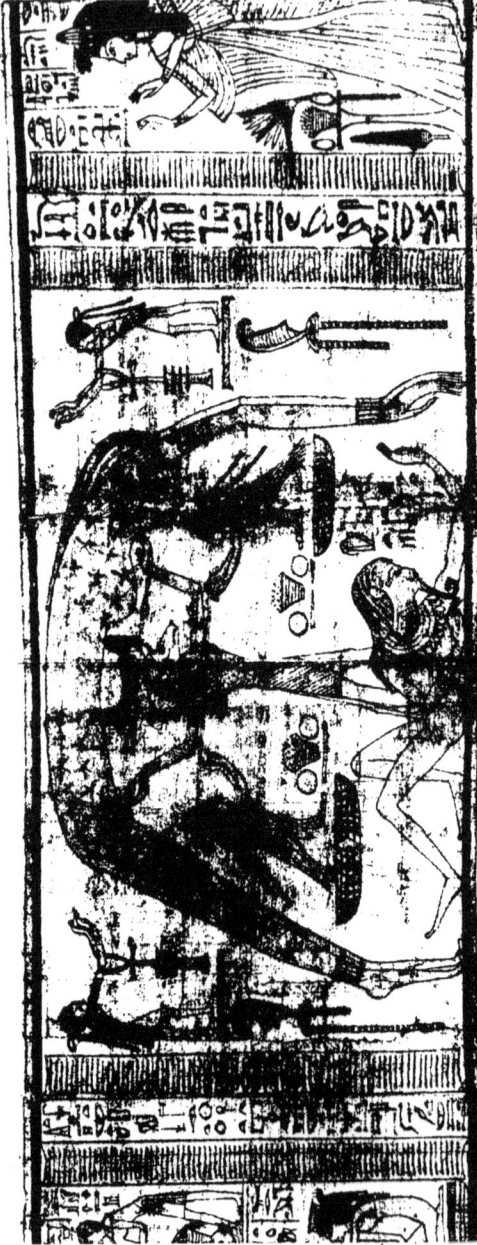

A Scene From The PAPYRUS OF NISITI – TA – NEBET – TAUI. See Minature Detail Next Page.

Note: The "STARS" shown on the body of Godess Nut were for the purpose of emphasizing that the "FEMALE" was in fact the "KEEPER OF HEAVEN". That the "CHAMBER OF LIFE" itself is in fact "HER WOMB"; all of this being part of the original "BLACK THEOLOGY" the plagiarists who wrote the OLD TESTAMENT, NEW TESTAMENT and/or QUR'AN distorted in the so-called "ADAM AND EVE" and/or "BEGINNING OF THE WORLD" allegory.

Note that God GEB is holding Goddess NUT at the "PILLARS OF THE WORLD" – her "REPRODUCTIVE ORGANS" and "MAMARY GLANDS", etc.; the same area from which "MAN" and WOMAN ORIGINATED.

CHAPTER XVI.

THE BOOK OF MAKING THE SPIRIT OF OSIRIS,[1] OR THE SPIRIT BURIAL.

THE FORMULA FOR MAKING THE SPIRIT OF OSIRIS[2] IN AKERTET, WHICH SHALL BE MADE (*i.e.*, RECITED) FOR THIS GOD, THE LORD OF ABYDOS, AT EVERY FESTIVAL OF OSIRIS, AND AT EVERY APPEARANCE [OF THE GOD] IN THE TEMPLES . . . . IT SHALL MAKE GLORIOUS HIS SOUL, IT SHALL STABLISH HIS BODY, IT SHALL MAKE HIS SOUL TO SHINE IN THE SKY, AND SHALL MAKE HIM TO RENEW HIS YOUTH EACH MONTH, IT SHALL STABLISH HIS SON HORUS UPON HIS COFFER. THIS FORMULA WAS RECITED BY THE SISTER [OF THE GOD]. IT WILL BENEFIT A MAN IF HE RECITETH IT, FOR HE SHALL BECOME A FAVOURED ONE OF OSIRIS UPON EARTH AMONG THE LIVING; HIS SON (?) SHALL BE ESTABLISHED IN HIS HOUSE EVERY DAY, AND HIS CHILDREN UPON THE [EARTH]. THIS FORMULA WAS RECITED BY ISIS AND HER SISTER NEPHTHYS, AND ALSO BY HER SON HORUS. AND IF IT BE RECITED FOR OSIRIS, IT WILL CAUSE THE SOUL OF THE DECEASED TO LIVE IN AKERTET EVERY DAY, IT WILL GLADDEN HIS HEART, AND WILL OVERTHROW ALL HIS ENEMIES; AND IT SHALL BE RECITED DURING THE IVTH MONTH OF THE SEASON AKHET,[3] FROM THE XXIIND DAY TO THE XXVITH DAY THEREOF. [Here follow the commemorative sentences.]

Come to thy house, come to thy house, O An. Come to thy house, O Beautiful Bull, the Lord of men and women, the beloved one, the lord of women. O Beautiful Face, Chief of Akertet, Prince, First of those who are in the Other World, are not [all] hearts drunk through love of thee (O Un-nefer) triumphant ? . . . .

---

[1] From a papyrus at Paris, a portion of which has been edited by Pierre, *Ét. Égyptologiques*, 1873), and see Brugsch, *Religion*, p. 626 ff.
[2] Or, commemorating Osiris.
Choiak.

Spirit Burial of Osiris

The hands of men and gods are lifted on high seeking for thee, even as those of a child [are stretched out] after his mother. Come thou to them, for their hearts are sad, and make them to appear as beings who rejoice. The lands of Horus[1] exult, the domains of Set are overthrown through fear of thee.

Hail, Osiris, First of those who are in the Other

---

1. From E.A. Wallis Budge's OSIRIS: THE EGYPTIAN RELIGION OF RESURRECTION, pages 44 - 45; like Sir J. Frazer's THE GOLDEN BOUGH [13 vols.], H.W. Smith's MAN AND HIS GODS, and Y. ben-Jochanan's AFRICA: MOTHER OF WESTERN CIVILIZATION say it is "religious bigotry."

World! I am thy sister Isis. No god hath done [for thee] what I have done, and no goddess. I made a man child, though I was a woman, because of my desire

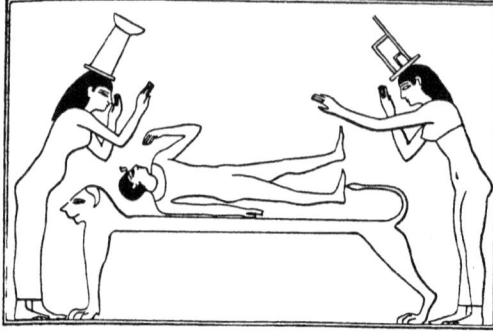

Isis and Nephthys bewailing the death of Osiris.
From a bas-relief at Philae.

to make thy name to live upon the earth. Thy divine essence was in my body; I placed him on the back of the earth (*i.e.*, brought him forth). He pleaded thy case, he healed thy suffering, he decreed the destruction of him that had caused it. Set hath fallen before his sword (or, knife), and the Smamiu fiends of Set have followed him. The throne of Ḳeb is to thee, O thou who art his beloved son!

Hail, Seker-Osiris! This calamity happened to thee in the primeval time. There have been made for thee mighty chambers in Ṭeṭṭu (Busiris). The god Uṭekh[2] embalmed thee and made sweet the smell of thee. The

---

[1] *I.e.*, the temple estates.　　　　[2] 🕭 ⬭ ⚬ 𓏭.

But in what respect do these differ from the following I have taken out of the teachings of the noted theologian Robertson Smith's major work- RELIGION OF THE SEMITES, which I have detailed in my own book - AFRICAN ORIGINS OF THE MAJOR "WESTERN RELIGIONS: Judaism, Christianity, Islam, page x:

> "No positive religion that has moved man has been able to start with a tabula rasa, and express itself as if religion were beginning for the first time, in form, if not in substance. The new system must be in contact all along the line with the older ideas and practices which it finds in possession. A new scheme of faith can find a hearing only by appealing to religious instincts and susceptibilities that already exist; and it cannot reach these without taking account of the traditional forms in which all religious feeling is embodied, and without speaking a language which men accustomed to these old forms can understand...."[1]

---

1. Failure to cite this fact would have been almost criminal. This is what is missing in most of our individual discipline type approaches to anything; we are too much chronological, and not quite enough analytically comparative; because of this we turned off millions of students daily.

Osiris and Human Sacrifice

1. The wicked cast head downwards into a pit of fire.
2. Enemies being burnt in a pit of fire.
3. The heads of the damned being burnt in a pit of fire.
4. The souls of the damned being burnt in a pit of fire.
5. The shadows of the damned being burnt in a pit of fire.

From the Book Ám-Ṭuat.

Extracted from E. A. W. Budge, OSIRIS: THE RE-
LIGION OF RESURRECTION, University Books,
Hyde Park, New York, 1961, p. 205. Could it be
from this "BLACK AFRICAN" source the LILY
"WHITE AFRICANS" and LILY "WHITE EURO-
PEANS" of the "CHRISTIAN RELIGION" got their
"HELL FIRE" and "DEVIL", et al?

JUDGEMENT SCENES DOWN THROUGH THE CENTURIES OF MAN'S RELIGION
From Africa, To Asia, And To Europe;
Finally To America

Ani and his wife watch his "HEART" being weighed against
the "FEATHER [symbol] OF MAAT" [truth]. The Divine Scribe
Toth, and the monster Am-mut at the far right await the verdict. [From The Egyptian Judgment Scene, Papyrus Of Ani,
British Museum, London; and Budge's Book Of The Dead; etc.]

OSIRIS PRESIDING OVER THE WEIGHING OF THE HEART:
A European VERSION of the scene above according to the
early European Christians who copied the African religion.

MICHAEL THE ARCHANGEL REPELS THE DEMONS WHO TRY
TO SEIZE THE FATEFUL SCALE OF THE "LAST JUDGMENT."
[From a 12th Century mosaic, Cathedral of St. Maria Assunta,
Torcello, Italy]. These Demons are also BLACK and HORNED.

LOVE: HEART or MIND - The Black Bible will have to clarify a grave semantical error that
is commonly the cause of many dissolutions of peaceful cohabitation and marriage, next only
to money and a few other material things...; that is:

'LOVING WITH ONE'S HEART.'

This greatest of all of the moderate myths in the various bibles was developed out of the
Greeks distortion of the indigenous Africans of the Nile Valley symbolism of the...

"WEIGHING OF ANI'S HEART AGAINST THE FEATHER OF TRUTH"

[Ani before Osiris]   [Gods in the Chamber of the Gods]

{Ani led by Anubis to   [Anubis weighing Ani's "Heart"   [Osiris leads Ani
his "Heart" weighed]   in the "Scale Of Justice Truth"]   to "Judgment Hall]

etc.[1] found in the BOOK OF THE DEAD and PAPYRUS OF ANI, Chapter XXXB, etc., etc., etc.

---

1. The hieroglyphic inscription tells of the deceased scribe named Ani getting his "Heart"
weighed preparatory to entering the "NETHER WORLD" [Heaven]. See English traslation by
Sir Ernest A. Wallis Budge's BOOK OF THE DEAD and PAPYRUS OF ANI, Chapter XXXB:

The following from page xv of the same volume helps in explaining another aspect of the frieze above taken from the EGYPTIAN BOOK OF THE DEAD and
PAPYRUS OF ANI; the two "SOULS" being further explained here, but better
seen on the following page; thus:

Left: The Ba or Heart-Soul
with the symbol of LIFE over
its body.
Right: The Ka or Spirit-Soul of
the deceased that depends upon
the Ba for continuance.

The "Ba" [black] represented the "SOUL IN ITS LIVING STATE;" whereas the "Ka" [white] represented the "SOUL OF THE DECEASED IN ITS DEATH STATE." From this aspect of the
"MAGICAL RELIGIOUS RITES" related to the DEATH of any pharaoh or high state official before everyone of the dynastic periods the MAGICIAN-PRIESTS developed the principle of the
"DIVINITY OF THE LIVING PHARAOH." And from this juncture the "DIVINE KINGSHIP"
principle among the upper-strata Africans of the Nile Valley High-Cultures entered into the
area of the "WORSHIP OF THE SUN DISC," which was also known as "Ra" or "God." All of
this happened more than three thousand [3,000] years before the first Asian Hebrew named
"ABRM" [or Abraham] was born in the City of Ur, Chaldea. This was almost another thousand

As he flies to heaven the gods of the West and the East, the South and the North, are invoked to receive him when he appears there.[1] Their reception of him is favourable, for he sails about on Qebḥu[2] freely. Being identified with Osiris, Horus, who regards him as his father, comes to his "two fingers," and salutes him, and causes him to rise like the great god on Qebḥu. And the gods say : Assuredly he is Horus, son of Isis, "assuredly he is the firstborn god, the son of Hathor, assuredly he is the seed of Ḳeb." Osiris orders that he is to be crowned as the second of Horus, and the Four Spirits who dwell in An have written the decree making them the two great gods in Qebḥu.[3]

Two sections of the text of Unás deal with the Ladder by which, according to a legend, Osiris ascended from earth to heaven; the first contains a series of addresses to divine powers, and the second refers to the setting up of the ladder. Thus we have : Homage to thee, Set-Âmenti,[4] mistress of Peter[5] of heaven, gift (?) of Thoth, mistress of the two sides of the Ladder,[6] open thou the way for

[1] Lines 572, 573.   [2] The celestial ocean.

[3] Lines 572–575.

The Ladder by which the deceased ascended from earth to heaven. From the Papyrus of Ani.

Note: This "ladder", excessively distorted and plagiarized in the Judaeo-Christian OLD TESTAMENT and NEW TESTAMENT, appears in many extracted papyri in this volume. This "ladder" equally affects the so-called "HOLY/SACRED SCRIPTURES" in the Muslim/Moslem QUR'AN. Yet, not one so-called "RELIGIOUS SCHOLAR" in either of these three religions ever told his/her parishoners that the "LADDER" was in fact first used "RELIGIOUSLY" in Africa as part of the Africans/Blacks' "BLACK THEOLOGY" that originated along the Nile Valleys and Great Lakes Region of Central Africa.
This "LADDER OF THE DEAD", or "STAIRWAY OF THE DEAD", etc. is commonly shown all over the pages of the BOOK OF THE COMING FORTH BY DAY AND BY NIGHT [Book Of The Dead and Papyrus Of Ani].

"JACOB'S LADDER",

or

THE STAIRWAY TO HEAVEN!

Ancient "Black Theology" called it STAIRWAY OF THE DEAD. All of this before Judaism, Christianity and Islam; and all before a single European nation existed. Of course Adam and Eve did not exist either.

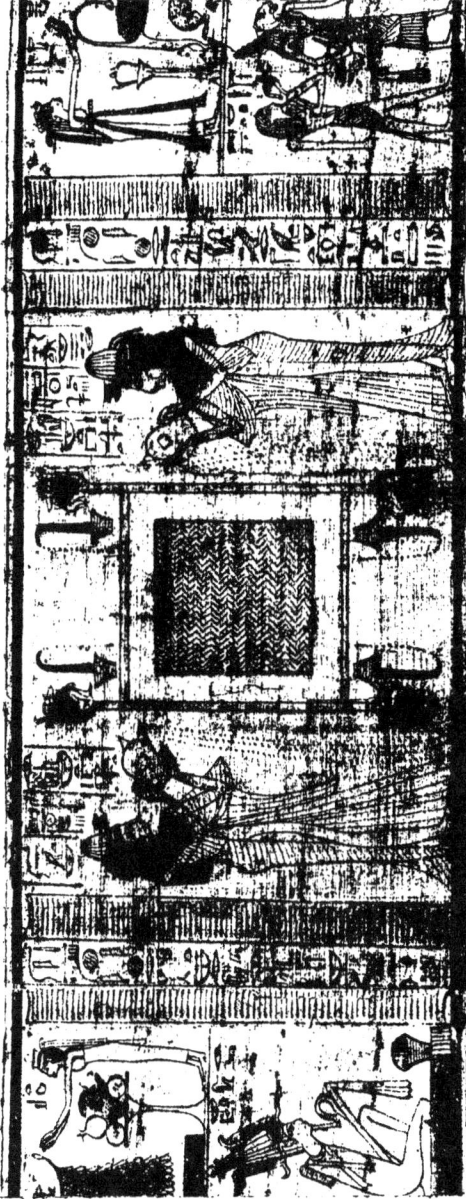

A scene from the PAPYRUS OF NISITI - TA - NEBET - YAUI of the
Book Of The Dead

Note: Be careful to observe in the middle of this frieze the "Hell Fire", as the two goddesses pour a fluid of life to temper the way of the deceased on his/her journey in search of the "Ankh/Key of Life" which is distorted to represent the present so-called "Christian Cross", etc. Also, that "Fruits" are always used as "Gifts For The Dead" instead of "Flowers". Libation/Spiritus Drink is equally used.

the deceased, set him on his way. Homage to thee, Nàu,[1] mistress of the marge of the Lake of Kha, open thou the way for the deceased, set him on his way. Homage to thee, O Nek, Bull of Rā with the four horns. Thy horn is in the West, thy horn is in the East, thy horn is in the South, thy horn is in the North. The meadow of thy horn is the Ǎment of the deceased, set thou him on his way. Certainly Ǎment is pure, [he] comes forth by thee to Baket. Homage to the Field of the Offering (Sekhet-ḥetep). Homage to the pasture which is in thee. The pasture of the deceased is in thee, pure offerings are in thee. Rā knots the Ladder for Osiris, Horus knots the Ladder for his father Osiris, going to his spirit. The one (Rā) [stands] on this side, and the other (Horus) on that, and the deceased is between them. Behold, he is the god whose seats are pure, he comes forth from a pure place, He stands up Horus, he sits down Set. Rā grasps his hand, a spirit in heaven, a body on earth. The flesh which has not [its] decree is helpless. His decree has the great seal, behold, his decree has not the little seal.[2]

Happy are those who see [the deceased], content be those who behold him, say the gods. Therefore this god comes forth in heaven, therefore the father comes forth in heaven. His souls are on him, his book is by his side, his words of power are in his mouth. . . . The divine Souls of Pe and the divine Souls of Nekhen, and the gods who belong to heaven, and the gods who belong to earth, come to him, and they lift him up on their hands. Come thou therefore to heaven, enter thou therein in its name of "Ladder." Heaven and earth have been given to him by Tem, Keb hath spoken concerning it. The Domains of Horus, the Domains of Set, and the Fields of Reeds praise thee in thy name of Khensu-Sept. The city Anu is as he is, god ; thy Anu is as he is, god ; Anu is as he is, Rā ; thy Anu is as he is, Rā. His mother is Anu, his father is Anu, he himself is Anu, born in Anu.[3]

[1] ~~~~ 𓇋 𓄿 𓅖 , the Ostrich-god ?

[2] Lines 579-583.   [3] Lines 584-592.

Extracted from E.A.W. Budge, OSIRIS: THE EGYPTIAN RELIGION OF RESURRECTION, University Press, Hyde Park, New York, pp. 124 - 125. Where did the JEWS get this symbol for their FIVE BOOKS OF MOSES? Was it not from their AFRICAN [Egyptian] HOSTS? Is this not one of the many reasons why the so-called "BLACK AFRICANS" must be removed from all of North Africa?

1. Why so-called "Black Theologians" have failed to inform their congragations about the above?

FORWARD:

Once again Professor Yosef ben-Jochannan has brought to surface some of
the suppressed information which is so critical for the SPIRITUAL GROWTH of African People everywhere, but particularly here in the United States of America and
other parts of the "NEW WORLD." And once again he has refused to follow the general
specified rigidly structural taboo established for what is historical to be separated
from that which is religious, political, social, economic, etc. This is obvious within
the framework of his incorporation of the sources he documented into the main text,
equal to the listing of works he used in the bibliography according to order of his research rather than according to ALPHABETICAL CHRONOLOGY.

Belaboring the issue of the quality of the sources used and information documented in this critically needed work will only take away from its importance in terms
of the "BLACK THEOLOGY" and "BLACK GOD" Professor ben-Jochannan reminds us
were part and parcel of everything that made our ancestors as "GREAT" as they were
in our motherland - ALKEBU-LAN - or "Africa." This is the reason I feel so honored
to be a party to its origin, production and final publication as the Research Assistant
of Professor ben-Jochannan with respect to the documentation for the Histo-religious
information in terms of events , dates, places, etc.

As Professor ben-Jochannan concentrates his energy and years of professional
expertise in communication through the written word on a level whereby the vast majority of the reading "African, African-American and African-Caribbean" public can
easily digest, it is just an extreme pleasure to be able to witness the effect it has on
so numerous an amount of his readers as the letters of commendation come into
Alkebu-lan Books Associates' offices daily.

Lastly; where else amongst African/Black authors of any discipline whatsoever
dealing with the "BLACK EXPERIENCE" is there such documentary proof challenging
the established order that belittles African People over the last two centuries with
every bit of DISTORTED and PLAGIARIZED information available to themselves?
What else, or who else, is challenging the "LILY WHITENESS" of the "BLACK
ORIGIN" of Judaism, Christianity and Islam? And, which other BLACK AUTHOR
amongst us - "BLACK PEOPLE" - is willing to suffer the consequences of ostricism
in bringing forward to the scrutiny of all the underlying DISTORTIONS and PLAGIAR-
ISMS inherent in "modern man's" presentations of the Jewish, Christian and Islamic

forms of antiquated taboos against "UNGODLY SEXUAL INTERCOURSE" because of their own puritanical idealism, superstition and allegorical myths inherited from Greek Mythology and other "Pagan" worships and their "Fire And Damnation" threats of an "Eternal Hell Fire" that will "Consume All Who Failed To Heed The One And Only True God" of their own creation?

The pleasure in reading this work and its accompanying volume - A BLACK THEOLOGY FOR THE IMMACULATE CONCEPTION AND VIRGIN BIRTH SYNDROME vs. OUR PYGMY ORIGIN - is too precious a treat for any in-depth revelation and detailed analysis here. Just respond in writing to the author your positive and negative reactions when you have completed both or either one. I am sure you will want to read all of Professor Yosef ben-Jochannan's other works. The manner in which he commenced the text on the following page should make you realize the depth of feelings and warmth the entire BLACK EXPERIENCE holds for him, and what it means for him to be able to lead his own BLACK PEOPLE by virtue of the proverbial addage that...

"THE PEN IS MIGHTIER THAN THE SWORD"....

-by-

George E. Simmonds [Research Associate to Yosef ben-Jochannan]
Adjunct Instructor of History, Malcolm-King College, Harlem,
New York City, New York.

Having given very serious thoughts to the numerous requests by my many African-American [BLACK] friends in the BLACK CLERGY to enter the CHRISTIAN, JEWISH, and/or MUSLIM/ MOSLEM MINISTRY, particularly as a "THEOLOGIAN", and being mindful of the fact that I had decided so many years ago to leave my own religion of ancestry... "JUDAISM/HEBREWISM", I had to ponder the basis for such a conclusion The first issue was the VALIDITY of the <u>source</u> of the information I was to use, and upon which I was to rest my entire confidence. This naturally brought me face to face with what it is; thus the <u>source</u>:

THE HOLY/SACRED SCRIPTURES or PENTATEUCH [Five Books Of Moses or <u>Old Testament</u>], KOIÑE BIBLE [<u>New Testament</u>], and/or QUR'AN [<u>Koran</u>].

But the specific <u>source</u> in this case, that which the "BLACK CLERGY" to whom I am to respond meant was the KOIÑE BIBLE [original "<u>New Testament</u>" written in ca. 50 - 100 C.E./A.D.] and all of the other various PROTESTANT and/or ROMAN CATHOLIC VERSIONS that followed until the present so-called "EVERY DAY LANGUAGE BIBLE", I found to have been the most DISTORT-ED from its original, to the extent that the following was written by Dr. Frank Crane in the "<u>Intro-duction</u>" of the so-called "LOST BOOKS OF THE BIBLE and FORGOTTEN BOOKS OF EDEN" - the works extracted from the ORIGINAL TEXTS/SCRIPTURES before, during and since the <u>Nicene Con-ference Of Bishops</u> in ca. 322 - 325 C.E./A.D.:

THE great things in this world are growths.
This applies to books as well as to institutions.

The Bible is a growth. Many people do not under-stand that it is not a book written by a single person, but it is a library of several books which were composed by various people in various countries. It is interesting to know how this library grew and upon what principle some books were accepted and some rejected.

Of course we may take people's word for the reasons why certain books were chosen, but it is always satisfac-tory to come to our own conclusions by examining our own evidence.

This is what this *Lost Books of the Bible* enables us to do. We can examine the books of the Scriptures which we have in the authorized version, and then in this book we can read those scriptures which have been eliminated by various councils in order to make up our standard Bible.

It is safe to say that a comparison of the accepted books with those rejected may be relied upon, for those books which were accepted are far superior in value to the others.

These others which are included in the *Lost Books of the Bible* comprise all kinds of stories, tales and myths.

No great figure appears in history without myths growing up about him. Every great personage becomes a nucleus or center about which folk tales cluster.

There are apocryphal tales about Napoleon, about Charlemagne, about Julius Cæsar and other outstanding characters.

It is impossible that a man representing so great a force as Jesus of Nazareth should appear in the world without finding many echoes of His personality in contemporary literature—many stories which grew up about Him as time elapsed.

What these tales and stories are, just how He appears to the fictional minds of His day and afterwards, it is interesting to note.

The above discovery was caused by my review of the charge by some know-nothings that:

"CHRISTIANITY IS THE WHITE MAN'S RELIGION".

And of course I wanted to examine at least one source written by a "BLACK AUTHORITY" who had nothing to gain as he analyzed the facts related to this area of "BLACK THEOLOGY". Thus it was that I remembered something about this, which I had totally enjoyed reading in Professor George G. M. James' STOLEN LEGACY [New York, 1954], page 178. He wrote:

> (6) *All the great religious leaders from Moses to Christ were Initiates of the Egyptian Mysteries*
> This is an inference from the nature of the Egyptian Mysteries and prevailing custom.
> (a) The Egyptian Mystery System was the One Holy Catholic Religion of the remotest antiquity.
> (b) It was the one and only Masonic Order of Antiquity, and as such,
> (c) It built the Grand Lodge of Luxor in Egypt and encompassed the ancient world with its branch lodges.
> (d) It was the first University of history and it made knowledge a secret, so that all who desired to become Priests and Teachers had to obtain their training from the Mystery System, either locally at a branch lodge or by travelling to Egypt.
> We know that Moses became an Egyptian Priest, a Hierogrammat, and that Christ after attending the lodge at Mt. Carmel went to Egypt for Final Initiation, which took place in the Great Pyramid of Cheops. Other religious leaders obtained their preparation from lodges most convenient to them.
> (e) This explains why all religions, seemingly different, have a common nucleus of similarity; belief in a God; belief in immortality and a code of ethics. Read Ancient Mysteries by C. H. Vail, p. 61; Mystical Life of Jesus by H. Spencer Lewis; Esoteric Christianity by Annie Besant, p. 107, 128-129; Philo; also read note (2) Chapter III for branch lodges of the ancient world.

Having examined the references Professor James used, I was still determined to become much closer in relationship to the actual "THEOLOGY" and "HISTORY" about the main "God Head" of the Christian Religion - JESUS "The Christ", of whom I found the following in SECTION XI, Chapter 47 and 48 of the AQUARIAN GOSPEL OF JESUS CHRIST, pages 87 - 89:

Life and Works of Jesus in Egypt

Jesus with Elihu and Salome in Egypt: Tells the story of his journeys. Elihu and Salome praise God. Jesus goes to the temple in Heliopolis and is received as a pupil.

AND Jesus came to Egypt land and all was well. He tarried, not upon the coast; he went at once to Zoan, home of Elihu and Salome, who five and twenty years before had taught his mother in their sacred school.

2 And there was joy when met these three. When last the son of Mary saw these sacred groves he was a babe;

3 And now a man grown strong by buffetings of every kind; a teacher who had stirred the multitudes in many lands.

4 And Jesus told the aged teachers all about his life; about his journeyings in foreign lands; about

the meetings with the masters and about his kind receptions by the multitudes.

5 Elihu and Salome heard his story with delight; they lifted up their eyes to heaven and said,

6 Our Father-God, let now thy servants go in peace, for we have seen the glory of the Lord;

7 And we have talked with him, the messenger of love, and of the covenant of peace on earth, good will to men.

8 Through him shall all the nations of the earth be blest; through him, Immanuel.

9 And Jesus stayed in Zoan many days; and then went forth unto the city of the sun, that men call Heliopolis, and sought admission to the temple of the sacred brotherhood.

10 The council of the brotherhood convened, and Jesus stood before the hierophant; he answered all the questions that were asked with clearness and with power.

11 The hierophant exclaimed, Rabboni of the rabbinate, why come you here? Your wisdom is the wisdom of the gods; why seek for wisdom in the halls of men?

12 And Jesus said, In every way of earth-life I would walk; in every hall of learning I would sit; the heights that any man has gained, these I would gain;

13 What any man has suffered I would meet, that I may know the griefs, the disappointments and the sore temptations of my brother man; that I may know just how to succour those in need.

14 I pray you, brothers, let me go into your dismal crypts; and I would pass the hardest of your tests.

15 The master said, Take then the vow of secret brotherhood. And Jesus took the vow of secret brotherhood.

16 Again the master spoke; he said, The greatest heights are gained by those who reach the greatest depths; and you shall reach the greatest depths.

17 The guide then led the way and in the fountain Jesus bathed; and when he had been clothed in proper garb he stood again before the hierophant.

CHAPTER 48

Jesus receives from the hierophant his mystic name and number. Passes the first brotherhood test, and receives his first degree, SIN-CERITY.

THE master took down from the wall a scroll on which was written down the number and the name of every attribute and character. He said,

2 The circle is the symbol of the perfect man, and seven is the number of the perfect man;

3 The Logos is the perfect word, that which creates; that which destroys, and that which saves.

4 This Hebrew master is the Logos of the Holy One, the Circle of the human race, the Seven of time.

5 And in the record book the scribe wrote down, The Logos-Circle-Seven; and thus was Jesus known.

6 The master said, The Logos will give heed to what I say: No man can enter into light till he has found himself. Go forth and search till you have found your soul and then return.

7 The guide led Jesus to a room in which the light was faint and mellow, like the light of early dawn.

8 The chamber walls were marked with mystic signs, with hieroglyphs and sacred texts; and in this chamber Jesus found himself alone where he remained for many days.

9 He read the sacred texts; thought out the meaning of the hieroglyphs and sought the import of the master's charge to find himself.

10 A revelation came; he got acquainted with his soul; he found himself; then he was not alone.

11 One night he slept and at the midnight hour, a door that he had not observed, was opened, and a priest in sombre garb came in and said,

12 My brother, pardon me for coming in at this unseemly hour; but I have come to save your life.

13 You are the victim of a cruel plot. The priests of Heliopolis are jealous of your fame, and they have said that you shall never leave these gloomy crypts alive.

14 The higher priests do not go forth to teach the world, and you are doomed to temple servitude.

15 Now, if you would be free, you must deceive these priests; must tell them you are here to stay for life;

16 And then, when you have gained all that you wish to gain, I

In the above it is obvious I could not find where JESUS entered Europe, nor where he was ever trained by a single European. Instead there is abundant evidence that he entered Alkebu-lan/Africa, and also his education in everything he knew from indigenous African [BLACK] professors, scribes, theologians, metaphysicians, magicians, astronomers, mathematicians, scientists, etc. - all of whom taught him in the MYSTERIES SYSTEM housed in the Grand Lodge of Luxor on the banks of the Nile River in Ta-Merry and Ta-Nehisi. This fact even included his own mother - "MARY" - according to the above Gospel. For the magnitude of the Grand Lodge Of Luxor and its extensive Subordinate Lodges I have included on the following page a picture of its ruin, and also a list of the Subs before the birth of MOSES and JESUS, and following their death ca. 3173 and 1978 years ago respectively. Of course within the "BLACK THEOLOGY" at the Grand Lodge of Luxor and its Subordinate Lodges was always the teachings about the IMMACULATE CONCEPTION" and "VIRGIN BIRTH" relative to JESUS, who later became "The Annointed/The Christ", was definitely only an

ORIGINAL MASONIC SIGNS, SYMBOLS, REGALIA, ETC. OF THE SUPREME SHRINE OF THE GRAND LODGE

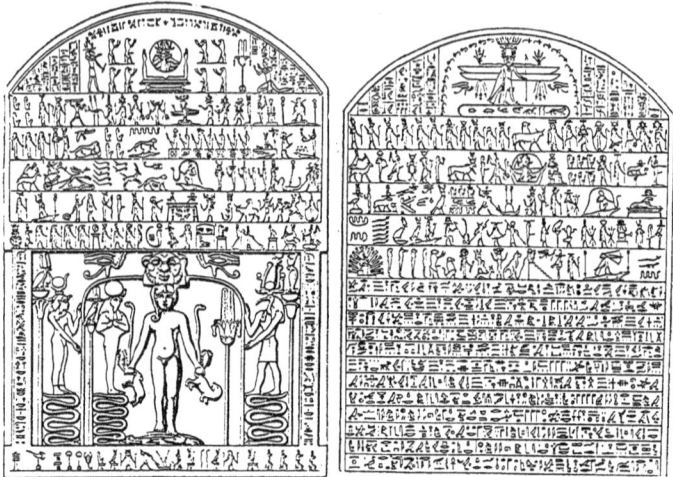

The colossal Cippus of Horus, which is commonly known as the "Metternich stele" (Obverse).

The colossal Cippus of Horus, which is commonly known as the "Metternich stele" (Reverse).

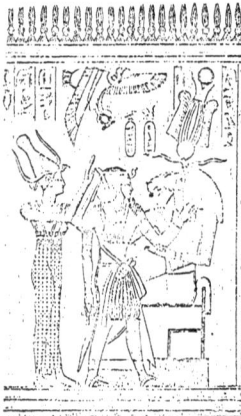

GRAND MASTER'S APRON AND COLLAR
Saïit presents the Pharaoh Amenothes III. to Khnûmû.
Drawn by Faucher-Gudin, from one of the bas-reliefs of the Temple of Khnûmû at Elephantine. This bas-relief is now destroyed.

Temple of Luxor — Upper-Egypt

SUBORDINATE LODGES OF THE GRAND LODGE OF LUXOR

1. Palestine [at Mt. Carmel]	10. Rhodes
2. Assyria [at Mt. Herman in Lebanon]	11. Delphi
3. Babylon	12. Miletus
4. Media [near the Red Sea]	13. Cyprus
5. India [at the banks of the Ganges River]	14. Corinth
6. Burma	15. Crete
7. Athens	16. Cush [Itiopi, Ethiopia]
8. Rome [at Elea]	17. Monomotapa [South Africa
9. Croton	18. Zimbabwe [Rhodesia]

LUXOR was destroyed by fire, burnt to the ground, in the year c. 848 B.C.E. It was set aflame by foreigners, who were jealous of the indigenous Africans [''Negroes,''et al] knowledge of the ''MYSTERIES'' taught in the Osirica - which included all of the above mentioned disciplines. [See John Kendrick's, ANCIENT EGYPT, Book II, p. 363; Eva B. Sandford's, THE MEDITERRANEAN WORLD, pp. 135 - 139; Yosef ben-Jochannan's, AFRICA: MOTHER OF ''WESTERN CIVILIZATION''. Chapter ??]

Note that the structure of the Grand Lodge shown above was the MAIN CENTER for all of the Subordinate Lodges where all of the Laws, Dogmas, Philosophies of the Mysteries System were created and developed to pass down to modern societies, etc.

CENTER OF THE MYSTERIES SYSTEM'S OSIRICA/ORIGIN OF FREEMASONRY

Columns of the RUINS OF THE GRAND LODGE OF LUXOR. It was completed by Pharaoh Amenhotep III, enlarged by Pharaoh Tut-ankh-Amon, and completed by Pharaoh Haremheb. Located at Thebes, Southern/Upper Egypt, Africa.

THE TEMPLE/TOMB OF AMON - MUT - CHONS, PERISTYLE OF
PHARAOH AMENHOTEP III, AND GREAT COURT AND PYLON OF PHARAOH RAMESES II, AT KARNAK

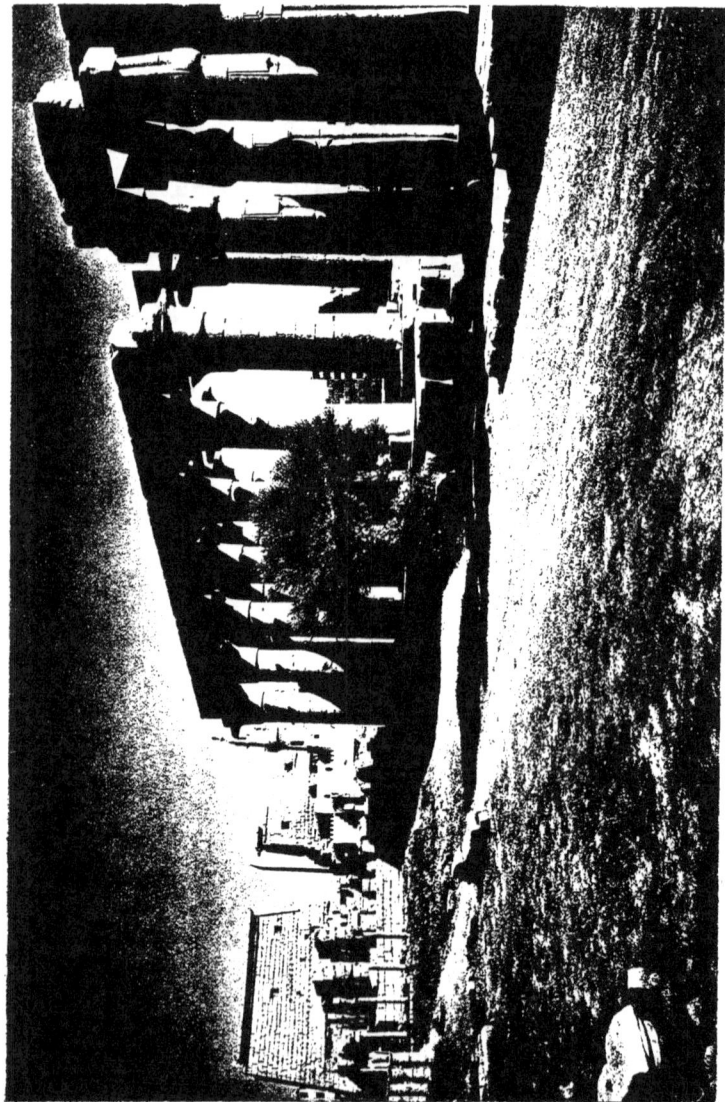

Note: The names "Amenhotep" and "Amenophis" were used to identify the same Royal Family in Egyptian History. "Akhenaten/Ikhnaten", etc. was given to the Pharaoh Amenhotep IV, son of the above Pharaoh. Akhenaten/Amenhotep IV became known as "The First Prince Of Peace" over 143 years before Jesus.

THE TEMPLE/TOMB OF PHARAOH AMON–MUT–CHONŜ and GREAT COURT AND PERISTYLE OF
PHARAOH AMENHOTEP III, AT KARNAK, EGYPT

A Scene And View From The East Looking West

THE TEMPLE/TOMB OF AMON AND GREAT HALL OF PILLARS OF PHARAOHS SETI I AND PHARAOH
RAMESES II [SON OF PHARAOH SETI I], AT KARNAK, EGYPT

THE "SACRED LAKE OF THE GODS" IN FOREGROUND
FIRST PYLON IN BACKGROUND

Note: It is most important to remember that most of these structures were conceived and built by southern
Africans before the arrival of the first European in history; the vast majority from Nubia, South of Egypt.

THE CEREMONIAL TEMPLE/TOMB OF PHARAOH THUTMOSES III,
AND THE TEMPLE OF AMON

Note: Thutmoses' Tomb in background, Temple of Amon at west foreground. Like all of the other Nile Valley structures shown in this volume, the artisans who built them were from the south.

Note: The above structures are labeled left to right with respect to royal names.

THE TEMPLE OF AMON, GREAT HALL OF PILLARS OF PHARAOH SETI/
SETHOS I, AND PHARAOH RAMESES II [SON OF SETI I], AND OBELISK OF PHARAOH
THUTMOSES/THUTMOSIS I

interpretation from the original story about ISIS AND HORUS - otherwise the BLACK MADONNA AND CHILD I have shown below as extracted from page 373 of my own book - BLACK MAN OF THE NILE AND HIS FAMILY:

Chapter X: MOTHER OF THE GODS OF MAN

MOTHER AND CHILD

Middle Kingdom Period, c. 2100 - 1675 B. C. E. [Bronze H, 5"]
Berlin-Charlottenburg, Staaliche Museen der Stiftung PreuBisher
Kulturbesitz, Egyptian Department.

In describing the above BLACK MADONNA AND CHILD statue the Museum
writers stated that "...BOTH HAVE TYPICAL NEGROID CHARACTERISTICS....."

All of this is further validated by the name in BLACK THEOLOGY that existed before European domination of CHRISTENDOM became a fact following the wars of Emperor Constantine ["the great"] and the manipulation of the Church Fathers of the IVth Century; names like the following assigned to HORUS, who was later called OSIRIS following his "DEATH" and "RESURRECTION" where he went and joined his father - the "ONE AND ONLY TRUE GOD...AMEN-RA":

In *The World's Sixteen Crucified Saviors*, Kersey Graves gave a list of these ancient savior gods with the dates of their reputed deaths. The list is as follows: Krishna of India (1200 B.C.), Sakia of India (600 B.C.), Tammuz of Syria (1160 B.C.), Wittoba of the Telingonese (522 B.C.), Iao of Nepal (622 B.C.), Hesus of the Celtic Druids (834 B.C.), Quetzalcoatl of Mexico (587 B.C.), Quirinius of Rome (506 B.C.), Prometheus of Greece (547 B.C.), Thulis of Egypt (1700 B.C.), Indra of Tibet (725 B.C.), Alcestos of Greece (600 B.C.), Atis of Phrygia (1170 B.C.), Crite of Chaldea (1200 B.C.), Bali of Orissa (725 B.C.), Mithra of Persia (600 B.C.).

OSIRIS, SON OF THE GODDESS ISIS

As numerous as the "NAMES OF HORUS" given, it is not to be forgotten that there were many hundreds more, all of which have been applied to many other characters in the PENTATEUCH [Old Testament] and NEW TESTAMENT. And all of them were equally associated with the following GODS whose teachings equally dominate what is today called "JUDAISM, CHRISTIANITY" and "ISLAM," not one of whom was any different in importance to YWH, JESUS ["the Christ"] and/or AL'LAH nor the so-called "SIXTEEN CRUCIFIED SAVIORS" listed on page x; thus some of the major GODS AND GODESSES FROM THE BOOK OF THE DEAD OF TA-MERRY:

Are the above facts, which I have presented from all kinds of documentary evidence, changing any of the claims that a "WHITE MAN'S CHRISTIANITY" has validity in terms of the PROPAGANDA being dispensed by those whose interests such charges

NAMES OF HORUS [or Osiris] ADOPTED FOR JESUS

HORUS I.—THE DIFFERENT NAMES OR ATTRIBUTES OF HORUS AND AMSU,* THE RISEN HORUS OR HORUS IN SPIRIT

Horus—The first Man-God
Horus—I. U. or I. A. U. = Jesus.
Horus—The Light of the World.
Horus—God of Life.
Horus—God of the Four Quarters, N. E. S. W.

Horus—God of the Pole Star.
Horus—God of Light.
Horus—Creator of Himself and Heir of Eternity.
Horus—Child of Isis.
Horus—King of the North and South.
Horus—Guide of the Northern Horizon.
Horus—In Spirit (Amsu).
Horus—Guardian of Sut.
Horus—Lord of Dawn and Evening Twilight.

Horus—Lord of the Northern and Southern Horizon.
Horus—Fettering Sut (or binding or chaining Satan).
Horus—Prince of the Emerald Stone.
Horus of the Triangle.
Horus—The Great One — The Mighty One.
Horus—The Great Chief of the Hammer or Axe.
Horus—Lord of Tattu.
Horus—The Blind.
Horus—The Tears of.
Horus—The Followers of.
Horus—The Feet of.
Horus—The Divine Healer.
Horus—The Master.
Horus—In the Tank of Flame (Baptiser with Fire).
Horus—The Good Shepherd with the Crook upon His Shoulder.
Horus—With Four Followers on the Mount.
Horus—With the Seven Great Spirits on the Mount.
Horus—As the Fisher.
Horus—As the Lamb.
Horus—As the Lion.
Horus—Of Twelve Years.
Horus—With the Tat (Cross).
Horus—Made a man at 30 years in his Baptism.
Horus—The Healer in the Mountain.
Horus—The Exorciser of Evil Spirits, as the Word.
Horus—Who gives the Waters of Life.
Horus—In the Bush of Thorns (as Unbu).
Horus—The Just and True.
Horus—The Bridegroom with the Bride in Sothis.

Horus—The Mighty One of the Teshert Crown.
Horus—In the Resurrection.
Horus—The Child-suckling.
Horus—The Great Spirit.
Horus—The Seven Powers of.

Horus—Of the Two Horizons.
Horus—As Hawk or Vulture or Eagle Hawk.
Horus—As Young Ear of Corn.
Horus—As Her-Shef or Khnemu—He who is on his Lake.
Horus—The Anointed Son of the Father.
Horus—The Red Calf (Type of Horus the Child).
Horus—In the Tree.
Horus—On the Cross.

Horus—As "I am the Resurrection and the Life."
Horus—Prince of Peace.
Horus—Who descends into Hades.
Horus—Lord of the Two Eyes or Double Vision.
Horus—The Manifesting Son of God.
Horus—As Child of the Virgin.
Horus—The Sower of Good Seed (and Sut the Destroyer).
Horus—Carried off by Sut to the Summit of the Mount Hetep.
Horus—Contending with Sut on the Mount.
Horus—One of Five Brethren.
Horus—The Brother of Sut, the betrayer.
Horus—Baptised with water by Anup.
Horus—Who exalted His Father in every Sacred Place.
Horus—The Weeper.
Horus—The Lifted Serpent.
Horus—In the Bosom of Ra (his Father).
Horus—The Avenger.
Horus—He who comes with Peace.
Horus—The Afflicted One.
Horus—The Lord of Resurrection from the House of Death.
Horus—As the type of Eternal Life.
Horus—The Child Teacher in the Temple (as Iu-em-Hetep).
Horus—As Ma-Kheru (the Witness unto Truth).
Horus—As the Lily.
Horus—Who came to fulfil the Law.
Horus—Walking the Water.
Horus—The Raiser of the Dead.
Horus—One with his Father.
Horus—Entering the Mount at Sunset to hold Converse with his Father.
Horus—Transfigured on the Mount.

Horus had two mothers : Isis, the Virgin, who conceived him, and Nephthysis, who nursed him.

He was brought forth singly and as one of five brothers.

Jesus had two mothers : Mary the Virgin, who conceived him, and Mary, the wife of Cleophas, who brought him forth as one of her children.

He was brought forth singly and as one of five brethren.

Horus was the Son of Seb, his father on earth.

Jesus was the son of Joseph, the father on earth.

Horus was with his mother, the Virgin, until 12 years old, when he was transformed into the beloved son of God, as the only begotten of the Father in heaven.

Jesus remained with his mother, the Virgin, up to the age of 12 years, when he left her " to be about his Father's business."

From 12 to 30 years of age there is no record in the life of Horus.

From 12 to 30 years of age there is no record in the life of Jesus:

Horus at 30 years of age became adult in his baptism by Anup:

Jesus at 30 years of age was made a man of in his baptism by John the Baptist:

Horus, in his baptism, made his transformation into the beloved son and only begotten of the Father—the holy spirit, represented by a bird.

Jesus, in his baptism, is hailed from heaven as the beloved son and only begotten of the Father. God—the holy spirit that is represented by a dove.

serve? Not at all. For as long as there is a presentation of a "CHRISTIAN GOD" like the PURE LILY WHITE JESUS shown below, and the JET BLACK DEVIL from whom He is rescuing a PURE LILY WHITE BLONDE that represents HOLINESS, there could be no manner of ways in which you can prove to those who are not aware of the source of such that "CHRISTIANITY" IS NOT "A WHITE MAN'S RELIGION"!

A WHITE Jesus Christ rescuing a PURE WHITE
CHRISTIAN SOUL -a white female- from a JET BLACK
DEVIL -a male . [From a MS in The John Rylands
Library, Manchester, Great Britain].

After saying all that I have so far, why should I still find it difficult to hear anyone say the following?:

"WHY SHOULD I GO TO CHURCH"?

This question has too frequently broken the silence of the otherwise quiet moments one could have in the midst of fellow BLACKS on any Sunday morning in the "HARLEMS" of the United States of America. But WHY? WHY did the BLACK MAN leave his WOMAN and CHILDREN in the "NEGRO CHURCH" to the total metaphysical brainwashing and control of "NEGRO/COLORED MEN" [or women] called "REVEREND" and/or "MINIS-TER", even "PROPHET" or "PROPHETESS", etc. ?

The latter question has plagued me for a few decades to date; as even in so-called "BLACK JUDAISM", which is totally MALE ORIENTED and DOMINATED to the nth degree, I found the same problem I would have a few years ago called "PHENOME-NAL" for a BLACK COMMUNITY [never "ghetto"] anywhere.

It would seem to me that the answer was in the lack of a truly BLACK THE-
OLOGY that I found missing in European and European-American dominated JUDAISM
and CHRISTIANITY, also Asian dominated ISLAM. Yet all three appeal to millions
upon millions of AFRICAN [Black] PEOPLE throughout the so-called "NEW WORLD,
WESTERN HEMISPHERE" and/or "AMERICAS" [including the Caribbean Islands]. For
it is in these so-called "GREAT RELIGIONS OF THE WESTERN WORLD," particularly the first two - "JUDAISM" and "CHRISTIANITY" that there is now a total absence of
the "BLACKNESS" and/or "AFRICANESS" that created them. But to the contrary, one
finds only the "WHITENESS" and/or "EUROPEANESS" that dominate "CHRISTENDOM"
since its takeover by Rome through the cunning manipulations of Emperor Constantine
["the great"] and his fellow Roman "Christians"[1]with their successful "RELIGIOUS
WARS" they maintained under the motto of "CHRISTIANIZING THE UNGODLY;" of
course with " THE SANCTION AND BLESSINGS OF THE ONE AND ONLY TRUE GOD
JESUS "Christ". Despite the fact that the Europeans and Asians, along with the Africans
who started the religions that produced "CHRISTIANITY, " had their own GOD, GODS,
GODESS and GODESSES, it made no difference to the religious bigots that committed all forms of PHYSICAL and CULTURAL GENOCIDE in the name of Jesus ['the Christ']
against their victims in order to secure their names on "CHRISTENDOM'S" roster.

But I was to question the newly found RELIGION to end all RELIGIOUS NEEDS
all of the BLACK PEOPLE OF THE WORLD had; this time it was "ISLAM, " the new
THEOLOGY with the latest "GOD" presented to the African People of the so-called
"DIASPORA" by those who were being influenced in this direction by the late Honor-
able Minister Malcolm X [Little, or el Haji Mallik Shabazz] for his then religious leader Prophet Elijah Mohammad [etc. , formerly Elijah Poole, now deceased]. Yet, it is an
African-American, so-called "LOST NEGROES"', version of the "RELIGION" and/or
"WAY OF LIFE" known as ISLAM, which Prophet Mohamed ibn Abdullah founded sometime during 622 C. E./ A. D. [or 1 A. H.: Year after the Hejira - the year Mohamet fled
Mecca to the outskirts of Medina where he established the Religion Of Islam]. And here
too I was to find no truly BLACK THEOLOGY; for these formerly "LOST NEGROES", who
since sanctified the "WHITE DEVIL" as an "ANGEL", cannot relate to an AFRICAN CON-
TINENT with any name, "AFRICA" being the most despised of all. Of course the following names shown on the map on the next page of this work will mean absolutely nothing to said African [BLACK] People, although ALKEBU-LAN is the most ancient any-

---

1. It is questionable if Constantine ever became a "Christian"; even on his death bed.

xli

one can document from the available written history:

Of AFRICA.
MAP
168 B.C.E.

A FRIC A, by the Ancients, was called *Olympia, Hefperia, Oceania, Coryphe, Ammonia, Ortygia,* and *Aethiopia.* By the Greeks and Romans, *Lybia* and *Africa.* By the *Aethiopians* and *Moors, Alkebu-lan.*

Note: The European colonialists, from the 15th through 19th century, C.E. refused to accept their ignorance of Africa's interior and made all sorts of map with waterways, mountains, nations and peoples which did not exist on the continent.

To these newly converted "MUSLIMS", who once prefered to be called "ASIATIC BLACK MEN AND WOMEN," the "ONLY TRUE DESIGNATION FOR AFRICA IS ASIA;" and of course the indigenous people are to be called like themselves - "ASIATIC [*?*] PEOPLE." It is only natural that the "ONE AND ONLY TRUE GOD" for the people of Alkebu-lan had to be the "ONE" they worship - "AL'LAH," who like all of the other information about everything else I have addressed myself to with regards to Alkebu-lan and her offsprings at home and in the "New World" only came into existence by virtue of Elijah Mohammad. But I am conditioned by experience in all of my writings from about the 1930's to demand DOCUMENTARY EVIDENCE to prove the latter allegation; and of course such was met with the following response before Mohammad's death:

"THAT IS ANOTHER OF THE WHITE MAN'S CORRUPTION
OF YOUR NEGRO MENTALITY MY BROTHER...;" etc.

This answer, never the less, bares no different stigma than that of JUDAISM'S RACIST IDENTITY of a so-called "SEMITIC RACE" that excluded the late Rabbi Matthew of the COMMANDMENT KEEPERS ETHIOPIAN HEBREW SYNAGOGUE shown on the next page.

xlii

addressing fellow BLACK ISRAELITES [or Jews, Hebrews, etc.],and handing out certificates of graduation in the HEBREW SCHOOL conducted by his congregation's female teachers and rabbis, et al.

Yet, not unlike the BLACK MUSLIMS, these same BLACK JEWS find it necessary to secure all of their so-called "SACRED" and "HOLY SCRIPTURES" similarly to the BLACK CHRISTIANS from publishing houses where the "HOLY SCRIPTURES" are written, edited and referenced solely by European, European-American, Asian and Asian-American producers of the various VERSIONS of the PENTATEUCH, NEW TESTAMENT and HOLY QUR'AN - each accordingly. It is at this juncture that we can clearly see the total dependency of the so-called "BLACK CHRISTIANS, BLACK JEWS" and "BLACK MUSLIMS" on the "HOLY SCRIPTURES" written, edited and referenced by WHITE and BROWN PEOPLES from Europe, European-America and Asia who do not in any manner shape or form identify with BLACK PEOPLE on the same racial and/ or ethnic criteria. For, not even one SOLITARY page shows a SOLITARY Black Man, Woman or Child's BLACK THEOLOGY! But is it not at this juncture that the Black Man consciously or sub-consciously decided to leave his BLACK FAMILY at the mercy of another? Certainly in neither of the HOLY SCRIPTURES or BIBLES I have mentioned could he find a BLACK IMAGE to relate to when he prayed to his ONE AND ONLY TRUE GOD. And if his GOD'S IMAGE was in no way, shape or form that of his own; what else was there to hold him in his BLACK [presently "Negro/Colored," etc.] CHURCH?

The answer for the BLACK MAN to return to his BLACK FAMILY who still remains in the "NEGRO/COLORED CHURCH" rests squarely in the "gut-bowels" of his own "BLACK THEOLOGY" which he must create and develop. This we should have observed when the late Prophet and Saint Martin Luther King, Jr.[1] failed to realize that

1. Male humans called "pope" make male and female "SAINTS" all the time in history.

the "NEGRO THEOLOGY" he preached and propagandized to a "GODLESS AMERICA, "
whose "WHITE THEOLOGY" is still comprised of a JUDAEO-CHRISTIAN [Graeco-
Romano] RACISM and RELIGIOUS BIGOTRY, would have caused his own MARTYR-
DOM. But how could he; when it was the same WHITE RACISM and EUROPEAN [white]
SEMITIC RELIGIOUS BIGOTRY like the following...

> Now I cannot beget the fourth son whose children I
> would have ordered to serve you and your brothers! There-
> fore it must be Canaan, your first born, whom they enslave.
> And since you have disabled me...doing ugly things in black-
> ness of night, Canaan's children shall be born ugly and black!
> Moreover, because you twisted your head around to see my
> nakedness, your grandchildren's hair shall be twisted into
> kinks, and their eyes red; again because your lips jested at
> my misfortune, theirs shall swell; and because you neglected
> my nakedness, they shall go naked, and their male members
> shall be shamefully elongated! Men of this race are called
> Negroes, their forefather Canaan commanded them to love
> theft and fornication, to be banded together in hatred of their
> masters and never to tell the truth! . . .

1. See Robert Graves and Robert Pattai's HEBREW MYTHS, New York, 1964, p. 121;
also a similar article in the OLD TESTAMENT OF THE HOLY BIBLE [Confraternity
Version]. Guild Press. New York [1952, 1955, 1961], footnote comments by Rev. Joseph
Grispino, S. M. L. commenting on the alleged RACIAL references by Noah; and Y. ben-
Jochannan's AFRICA: MOTHER OF "WESTERN CIVILIZATION, " Alkebu-lan Books Asso-
ciates, New York, 1971.

that is equally behind the "AUTHORITY" at Boston University, Boston, Massachusettes
which gave him the "DOCTORATE DEGREE" in EUROPEAN THEOLOGY he, as all of
the BLACKS who were trained {"educated"] by and in WHITE THEOLOGIANS'nest ? And
although this is no personal reflection on anything wrong on the part of this BLACK
PROPHET and/or SAINT; never the less, it should be a reminder to those who followed his leadership that the "IMAGE" of one's MASTER constantly revered as one's GOD
cannot result in "FREEDOM" in any manner whatsoever other than that which a SLAVE
MENTALITY considers to be "FREEDOM." For "GOD" is only REAL in the IMAGE of
the believer. Thus only a "GOD" that is materialized in the "IMAGE" of the people who
worship HIM, HER, IT, etc. will serve them honestly. And in order to have this type
of "BLACK GOD" the BLACK MAN must have a totally BLACK PHILOSOPHY for his
BLACK THEOLOGY which he must inculcate into his BLACK CHURCH to meet the every
needs of the BLACK DIVINITY, who must look down from the stained glass windows and
paneled walls behind the pulpit where the BLACK clergyman stands while preaching and
teaching to a BLACK CONGREGATION. Thus it is that I went to the SOUTHLAND in
search of a BLACK THEOLOGY in the BLACK SEMINARIES; only to find not one.

THEOLOGY MAINTAINS RACIAL/ETHNIC TRUTH AT ALL TIMES
[Extracted from S.G.F. Brandon's "Religion In Ancient History"]

An Islamic version: Gushtasp, Zoroaster's royal patron, is entertained by the legendary King Isfandiyar; a Persian miniature

"Before the cock crows. . ." An early depiction of Peter's denial of Jesus (from a 4th cent. sarcophagus in the Lateran Museum, Rome)

Top from page 207. Bottom from page 226. Europeans are WHITE, Asians BROWN/YELLOW, etc.

In the pursuit of all that I am teaching here with regards to "BLACK THEOLOGY", I must bring to your attention the following by Evelyn Walker, who was my Graduate Student at Africana Studies and Research Center, Cornell University, Ithaca, New York. It is an extract titled - "THE LAW OF OPPOSITE: AN INTERPRETATION"; a Final Term Paper submitted for the Fall Semester of 1974 C.E., and published with two other students and myself in a pamphlet - Understanding The African Philosophical Concept Behind The "Diagram Of The Law Of Opposites";[1] thus she states:

The deification of man is not a new phenomena. It has existed since the beginning of man in the Nile Valley and other areas of Africa. If, as Frazier has stated, man in his early years worshipped stones and trees, the attributes of such objects were distinctly human [Frazier, THE GOLDEN BOUGH, Vol. I, p. 89]. He has thus personified that which he calls "god [s]" since time immemorial. Is this not the way it should be? Man, in judging all that was around him, could use only himself as a measuring stick. It is only natural that his ideas of divinity reflect what he thought things to be.

It has been stated that the religions of Western Europe as well as Hinduism and Islam of Asia have their foundations in the Egyptian Mystery [Mysteries] System, more specifically, in THE LAW OF OPPOSITES. It is apparent that on examining the theology of Egypt, India and Greece, there are striking similarities in the religious tenets. Some of these similarities will be focused upon in an attempt to further clarify the presumption that just as man came out of the Nile, so did his religion.

The Egyptian religious system has been called by some authors a polytheism, which makes it unlikely, if not impossible, that the monotheistic religions could have developed out of it. Recent works such as that of professor ben-Jochannan have aided in dissipating this accusation [Dr. Yosef ben-Jochannan], BLACK MAN OF THE NILE AND HIS FAMILY]. Comparative study between the Jesus/Mary/Joseph story and that of Horus/Isis/Osiris have shown that the two bear a striking resemblance, allowing, of course, for factors of geography and history. Further, comparison of Osiris and Adonis by Frazier in the GOLDEN BOUGH also show similarity in the birth and death of the two. What are the implications of this? At worst, the three are coincidental; at best and more likely, the stories are different versions of the same occurance with Osiris being the original story. Thus, if Egypt was polytheistic, so was Rome.

If there is a better way in which to close this aspect of "BLACK THEOLOGY", I do not know how. For I am too proud of my student's ability to capture her professor's insight....Amen-Ra.

1. Pages 22 - 27, Alkebu-lan Books Associates, New York, 1975; Co-authors - Y. ben-Jochannan, E. Walker, C. Birdsong and D. Lee Cobb.

A "glossary" is not always necessary, but in all cases one cannot hurt, instead it can always help. In this situation a "glossary" is compulsary. Why? Because this volume contains words that will mean different things to different people according to their own cultural, racial, and/or religious background. Moreso, this volume contains words the author has debunked as having solely "racist" meaning, and as such when used must be clearly defined in quotation marks or the like. For example: The word "heathen" has no validity in terms of a single African indigenous to the continent of Africa, being that Africans have always had "GOD" in the concept of an all-encompassing unseen force/power no different to the Judaeo-Christian-Islamic JEHOVAH, JESUS ["the Christ"] and AL'LAH. For this reason, and so many others, a "GLOSSARY" follows; thus:

GLOSSARY:[1]

Religion... the structured worship of a deity/deities and/or other entities, etc. which people believe is solely responsible for their being.

God/Deity... that for which religion was created; the entity we worship; that which is resposible for everything that exists.

Dogma... rules or other dictations handed down from a religious authority of a religious nature, etc.

Theologian... one who studies and teaches religion and theism, etc.

Rabbi... a religious leader and teacher of Judaism - the Hebrew/Israelite religion, and who also minister's its sacrements, etc.

Minister... the equivalent of a rabbi, but with more power, of the Christian Religion.

Priest... same as the above but of the Roman Catholic Church, etc.

Imam/Emam... the spiritual leader of the Moslems/Muslims.

Judaism... the religion of the Hebrews/Israelites [misnomered "Jewish People", etc.]

Christianity... the religion of the followers of Jesus "the Christ" - Christians, etc.

Islam... the religion of the Moslems/Muslims.

Theosophy... the study of theism/God/the Deity, etc.

Culture/Civilization... a way of life for a compact of people living under one set of laws that govern all of them.

Pygmy/Pigmy... a derogatory name placed upon an African People who named themselves "TWA".

Witch Doctor... a derogatory name placed upon African Doctors of Herbology/Herbal Medicine plac.. by European colonialist so-called "Christian Missionaries", and others.

Race... the distinguishing physical characteristics between different species of animals,

Myth... a folkloric/traditional story of unknown authorship.

Allegory... a story with various meanings which may or may not be true.

Distort... to wilfully change anything for the purpose of deceiving anyone. Create a false appearance.

Plagiarization... to claim or otherwise reduce to ones ownership that which in fact belongs to another person or persons; somewhat similar to the above, but not necessarily with the same characteristics given here.

ad infinitum... Latin for forever and forever, or almost without ending, etc.

Prophet... one who has certain religious powers, allegedly, and can tell/prophesize the future, etc.

Egyptologist... one who studies and teaches the culture, etc. of Egypt, Northeast Africa of ancient

---

1. All of these words are listed according to their chronological appearance [page by page] in the general text of this work. Some of the interpretation will be totally coloquial; solely for the purpose that this volume is prepared for the general public of African-[BLACK]-Americans primarily.

[glossary continued]:

Palaeontologist...
Version... something very close to the original, but not the original.
Pervert... to change and make distasteful, rejectful, deceitful, etc.
Sacred... that which is Godly to a particular group, religion, etc.
Holy... similar to "Sacred",
Bible... a book of sacred writings/scriptures, etc. related to a deity/deities, etc.
Ethnocentrism... that which is based solely upon ethnic consideration.
Fossil-Human... ancient remains of human beings found inbeded deep below the earth surface.
Alkebu-lan... the oldest know name for the continent the Greeks called Africa.
Concept... an idea or method of doing something.
Principle... a set of law or rule by which something is to be done/accomplished.
Papyrus... the Greek name for original "paper" created by the Africans of Egypt and other Nile
              Valley High-Cultures; made from the "papyrus plant".
Power/Force... energy, energetic control and causeability, to cause action, etc.
Amulet... a "sacred" charm to be worn around the neck.
Talisman... a "sacred/holy" object to be used similarly to the above.
Indigenous... native to the soil, original occupant of the land, etc.
Convert... to change from one set of religious teachings and/or God concept to another.
Doctrine... rule or edict establish by any source of authority; in this case religious authority.
Belief... to have faith in anything for any reason whatsoever that your feeling is correct.
Apartheid...
Pan-Africanism... the philosophy of a common nationalism for all people of African birth and/or
              origin in order to unite the peoples and countries of Africa.
Nationalism... adhearance to a philosophy of common ownership between a certain people of a nation
Sect... an off-shoot of a specific religious group or organization, etc.
Heritage... that which one receives by virtue of inherritance historically.
Freedom... the ability to move freely within a given society according to common understanding be-
              tween the ruled and the ruler, etc.
Truth... that which is commonly agreed upon within any group as the fact.
Independence... the freedom of any nation to rule itself without interference from other nations.
Colonialism... where one national group of people forces control upon another by occupying their
              land, etc. with armies generally.
Neo-colonialism... where a foreign nation assumes control over another by using the citizens of
              said nation to work in the interest of the foreign state mostly for financial
              rewards, etc.
Violence... to disrupt and cause chaos, disturbance of the peace by force and disorder, etc.
Traditional... a way of doing things proven satisfactory over a period of time of very long duration.
Rites...
Rituals...
Genocide... the extermination of a people by another solely because of their differences, etc.
Chattle Slavery... the physical imposition of servitude without pay or freedom to move freely; and
              to keep said person in physical restraint to the point of committing physi-
              cal damage to the person, etc.
Integration... the physical fusing of two seperate things into one as a recognizeable whole, etc.
Militant... one who is unusually aggressive by virtue of idealism with respect to something general-
              ly different to that which is commonly accepted as being normal.
Diaspora... people in a foreign land by virtue of captivity or other method of force against their will
Blessing... good fortune caused by "divine grace" and/or "rituals", etc.
Curse... bad fortune caused by divine displeasure and/or rituals of ill fate, etc.

xlviii

Born Again Christian...a fanatical believer in the Christian Religion/Faith as stated in its teachings

Christ...originally "Messiah" [Hebrew], Crystos [Greek], Christ/Annointed [English], etc.

Madonna...Holy or Sacred Mother of any Deity/God, etc.

Image...a face or form of anything, etc.

Semitic...related to the son of Noah named Shem/Sem in the biblical story of the Flood/Great Deluge as stated in the Book Of Genesis of the Jewish Bible/Old Testament.

Hamitic...related to the youngest son of Noah of the above story, etc.

Caucasian...people who originally came from the Caucasus Mountains between Europe and Asia.

Immaculate...pure, clean, true, without blemish, etc.

Virgin...original, first, etc.; or biologically a female with her hymen intact, etc.

Negro...a derrogatory name given to Africans by Portuguese slavers during the 16 - 17th century.

Coloured...a racist term of inferiority for the very light-skinned offspring of parents who are of so-called "MIXED-PARENTAGE" [White and Black, etc.]

Ministry...the office of a clergyman/clergywoman of any religious sect, etc.

Holy Land...the geographic location of some specific religious occurance related to a miracle or spiritual happening not explainable by the people who believe in it.

Scriptures...in religion related to the religious writings about the Deity/God of said group, etc.

Capitalism...an economic system [also called "free enterprise"] whereby capital investors share the majority of the wealth produce from production after expenses for materials, labour, management, sales handling, etc.

Socialism...an economic system whereby the majority of the interest resulting from production after gross costs, etc. are distributed back to the workers by means of salaries and other benefits with the other part going to the government/state and back into production for maximum employment, etc.

Communalism...an economic system used by African nations before, and after, the arrival of the European colonialists to Africa who killed it by introducing "capitalism"; a state of economic distribution according to human needs rather than one's ability to produce more than another, condemned by many who adopted its basic structure as being "a primitive form of socialism/communism", etc.

Marxism...the study of the writings of Karl Marx, generally acclaimed as the author of "modern socialism" from and allegedly "scientific process", etc. developed during the 19th century C.E./A.D.

Arab...originally an indigenous/native Asian of the Arabian Peninsula of Western Asia.

Devil...an evil deity/god mentioned specifically by Christian teachings and other related works; the bad/wicked entity who supposedly causes people to do wrong things, etc.

Create...to bring into being, the original perpetuator of anything or anyone, etc.

Tithing...the tax of religious persons by their religious institutions for the support of the clerical hierarchy, physical properties of the institution, and other related matters.

Brainwashing...the process of consentrated propaganda forced upon anyone at the exclusion of all other information to the contrary, etc.

Missionary...a person who becomes obcessed with his/her idealism that the rest of the world who do not have his/her type of religion, God/Deity and theosophy will be lost into damnation, etc. "Christians" believe said "Lost people will wind-up in Hell with the Devil", etc.; a thought not to disimilar to the Muslims.

Caucasian...a person whos traces his/her ancestral beginnings to the Caucasus Mts. between Asia and Europe. Today called "dark-skinned" and/or "white-skinned", etc.

---

1. All of the above listed words/terms on this page and on pages vi - vii meanings are the only ones to be used in this volume, irrespective of anyother meaning you will find in any dictionary. These are the usage the author used in the preparation of the entire text; other usage will prove in error.

CREDIT:

It is very difficult to determine just who, among so many others that affect your work, must be especially singled out for "CREDIT". In this case I found the task very easy, as the persons to be credited have been so very instrumental in the final outcome of this volume; thus:

> To my always "right hand man" Professor George E. Simmonds for his checking and research of the documents presented; my student understudy Gregory Hardy for assisting in the general reading of the manuscript with criticism, and his general office work; Virginia Mixon, a most gracious volunteer, for her day to day editing and proofreading of the manuscript in its so many stages of development; and of course Dr. Mary Lewis for typing and critical reading of the final manuscript.

> Very special "credit" is due Dr. Arthur Lewis, M.D. and his wife Dr. Mary Lewis [mentioned above] for their most timely financial contribution in order to make this and other works available to the general reading public who has for so many years depended upon Alkebu-lan Books Associates for the type of documents this volume provides. Without these two lovely African-[BLACK]-Brother and Sister this work would not have been able to reach the printer, muchless the reader.

> Brother Gil Noble of Channel 7, A.B.C. Television's "LIKE IT IS" program must be categorized equally, for it is due to my appearances on this program which made Miss Mixon and the Lewis' become aware of your author and his works. Of course Brother Noble is without this comment a credit to African/ Black People throughout the entire world - the so-called "DI-ASPORA" in particular.

This work will be followed by another in the same general theme of "BLACK/AFRICAN THE-OLOGY". However, it is dealing with the most recent one hundred and eighty degree [180⁰] about face our former so-called "BLACK POWER MILITANTS" of the 1960's A.D./C.E. have taken to the safe hiding place of "NEGRO/COLORED RELIGION", all based upon either ARAB-ASIAN and EUROPEAN-AMERICAN "BROWN" and/or "WHITE" THEOLOGY.

1

BASIC-FACTS HIDDEN FROM THE BLACK
SEMINARIANS AND THE BLACK CLERGY:

I ventured southwards from my Harlem, New York City, New York base
with nothing else but greatest enthusiasm; once again I was finally going to achieve
one of my greatest desires - LECTURE IN A BLACK SCHOOL. I was equally as ex-
cited to realize that I had to meet "heads-on" with the "NEGRO" and/or "COLORED"
supercilious structure that controlled an all"NEGRO/COLORED" SEMINARY today in
the latter part of the 20th Century C.E. This was no earlier than during 1973-74 C.E.

When I visited Payne College Seminary of Wilberforce University in Xenia,Ohio;
Interdenominational Theological College [ITC] in Atlanta, Georgia; Shaw Divinity School
in Raleigh, North Carolina, and quite a few others, all of them on a non-official invi-
tational basis in order not to have been guided to what my official hosts and hostesses
would have wanted my attention to be focused on, I was more than disappointed; I was
in fact disgusted. Let me hasten to add that my disgust was not caused by the APATHY
of those at the helm of the SEMINARY, for such would be far from the truth in either
case. The ironic insult is in the fact that not a solitary one of them had, has, and apparently if left alone will ever have in the future, its own BLACK THEOLOGY. Quite
to the contrary, they - each and everyone of them - have adopted, accepted and per-
fected a WHITE THEOLOGY with its WHITE HOLY FAMILY that includes their LILY
WHITE BLONDE, BLUE EYE, GOLDEN HAIRED and DOVE OF PEACE passive Jesus
"the Christ." Yet all of them maintained in their TEACHINGS and PREACHINGS from
pulpits located directly under stained glass windows and wall-panels with their radiant
exhibit of Michaelangelo's LILY WHITE HOLY FAMILY [comprised of his own UNCLE,
AUNT-IN-LAW and COUSIN he used for the models he painted for Pope Julius IVth on
the ceiling of the Cistene Chapel of Saint Peter's Basillica in Rome, all of which began
during ca. 1509 C.E. and was completed in ca. 1511 C.E.] that:

"GOD [meaning Jesus "the Christ"] HAS NO COLOR."

But if "God Has No Color;" why does each new and/or existing panel and stained glass
window in each and every "NEGRO/COLORED SEMINARY" wind up with the same type
of LILY WHITE JESUS, ANGELS and HEAVEN like the picture at the top of the following page, but not that below it; all of which is equally portrayed in each and every
CHURCH headed by each and every "NEGRO/COLORED" graduate seminarian from
each and every "NEGRO/COLORED" seminary ?

1

"THE CRUCIFIXION" by Andrea Mantegna, ca. 1431-1506 C.E. [From a painting in the Louvre, Paris, France]. The ultimate in PURE WHITE CHRISTIANITY.

JESUS "THE CHRIST"
Shown as the "Good Shepherd" in all of His blackness.
Favourite of the early Christians of Europe when all
pictures and statues of JESUS were shown "BLACK."
[From a 4th Century C.E. mosaic pavement at
Aquileia].

The answer was quite apparent as I saw the first piece of material used in BRAINWASHING our "Young, Black, Beautiful and Gifted" African-American men and women to end up "NEGRO" and/or "COLORED" copies of BILLY GRAHAM, POPE JOHN, BISHOP PIKE, REV. HENRY FOSDICK, REV. RICHARD WARD WEIR, REV. GARNET TED ARMSTRONG, REV. NORMAN VINCENT PEALE, et al.[1] All of these, and more, have thousands of their SERMONS being ingested and regurgitated as examples of "GREAT TEACHINGS OF CHRISTENDOM'S WORLD OF JESUS", etc.

1. Very seldom, if ever, "Negro Clergymen/women" quote "Black Theologians'" works.

2

Yet, I tried desparately to find a solitary SERMON by a single BLACK clergyman or clergywoman held in equal esteem as anyone of the so-called GREAT WHITE FATHERS I have already named. Just imagine;

THERE WAS NOT A SINGLE ONE!

But, how could there be A SINGLE ONE when in most of the so-called "NEGRO/ COLORED SEMINARIES" there still appear in the HYMNALS they use for "DEVOTIONAL SINGING" songs with the following words:

"LORD, MAKE ME WHITER THAN SNOW, MORE THAN SNOW"?

Just imagine a "NEGRO/COLORED [supposedly 'black'] THEOLOGIAN" requesting of his YOUNG, GIFTED, BEAUTIFUL AND BLACK SEMINARIANS that they sing with all their deepest passion this RACIST ANTHEM without his being conscious of the impact on the minds of his charges! It should not be difficult, non-whatever; as most of them order this type of song be sung at least three times each year in ALL BLACK CONGREGATIONS of ALL BLACK NEIGHBORHOODS, as it is the FAVORITE for so many of our graduate seminarian ministers and non-graduate "hole in the wall storefront" compatriots of the gospel - particularly when they desire to free themselves and their own parishoners from their so-called...

"BLACK SIN" and "BLACK CURSE INHERITED FROM HAM"....

All of this we can see each and every "COMMUNION SUNDAY" as we make our sanctuary PURE AS THE LILY WHITE MAN, DISCIPLES, ANGELS, etc. who constantly look down on us; dressed no doubt in their equally LILY WHITE GARMENTS, the same COLOR we have used to cover most everything in sight except those that are already LILY WHITE. Why? We know not of the "BLACK CHRIST" of Ethiopia in this volume.

Out of all of this, how can a "BLACK THEOLOGY" even get born, much less survive in this quagmire of PURE LILY WHITE THEOLOGY which African People have been brainwashed into believing was...

"ORDAINED BY GOD" [Jesus the Christ]...?

How could those who are to develop it think of it when their minds are so dominated in their LILY WHITE RIGHTEOUSNESS? How could it get born out of the minds of the new young BLACK seminarians who could look around themselves and plainly see that AFRICAN [Black] PEOPLE need a JET BLACK GOD of their own who knows and love us; just because WE are ourselves? One like the following GOD who loved us in Alkebu-lan, and others shown throughout this work:

3

[symbols imposed by <u>Yosef ben-Jochannan</u> for effect]

Did this GOD not make...

"MAN IN HIS OWN IMAGE"...

like the Judaeo-Christian GOD-HEAD <u>Jehovah</u> or <u>Jesus</u>["the Christ"]for whom the following was written about ca. 700 - 500 B.C.E., according to GENESIS ii : 1 - 25?:

2 THUS the heavens and the earth were finished, and all the host of them.

2 And on the seventh day God ended his work which he had made; and he rested on the seventh day from all his work which he had made.

3 And God blessed the seventh day, and sanctified it: because that in it he had rested from all his work which God created and made.

The manner of the creation

4 ¶ These *are* the generations of the heavens and of the earth when they were {created, in / created. In} the day that the LORD God made the earth and the heavens,

5 {And every plant of the field before it was / when no plant of the field was yet} in the earth, and {every herb of the field before it grew: / no herb of the field had yet sprung up—} for the LORD God had not caused it to rain upon the earth, and *there was* {not a man to till the ground. / no man to till the ground; }

6 But there went up a mist from the earth, and watered the whole face of the {ground. / ground—}

7 {And / then} the LORD God formed man *of* the dust of the ground, and breathed into his nostrils the breath of life; and man became a living soul.

The garden of Eden, and
the river thereof

8 ¶ And the LORD God planted a garden eastward in Eden; and there he put the man whom he had formed.

9 And out of the ground made the LORD God to grow every tree that is pleasant to the sight, and good for food; the tree of life also in the midst of the garden, and the tree of knowledge of good and evil.

4

10 And a river went out of Eden to water the garden; and from thence it was parted, and became into four heads.

11 The name of the first *is* Pison: that *is* it which compasseth the whole land of Havilah, where *there is* gold;

12 And the gold of that land *is* good: there *is* bdellium and the onyx stone.

13 And the name of the second river *is* Gihon: the same *is* it that compasseth the whole land of Ethiopia.

14 And the name of the third river *is* Hiddekel: that *is* it which goeth toward the east of Assyria. And the fourth river *is* Euphrates.

15 And the LORD God took the man, and put him into the garden of Eden to dress it and to keep it.

16 And the LORD God commanded the man, saying, Of every tree of the garden thou mayest freely eat:

The tree of knowledge

17 But of the tree of the knowledge of good and evil, thou shalt not eat of it: for in the day that thou eatest thereof thou shalt surely die.

18 ¶ And the LORD God said, It is not good that the man should be alone; I will make him an help meet for him.

19 And out of the ground the LORD God formed every beast of the field, and every fowl of the air; and brought *them* unto Adam to see what he would call them: and whatsoever Adam called every living creature, that *was* the name thereof.

20 And Adam gave names to all cattle, and to the fowl of the air, and to every beast of the field; but for Adam there was not found an help meet for him.

The making of woman and the institution of marriage

21 And the LORD God caused a deep sleep to fall upon Adam, and he slept: and he took one of his ribs, and closed up the flesh instead thereof;

22 And the rib, which the LORD God had taken from man, {made he / he made into} a woman, and brought her unto the man.

23 And Adam said, This *is* now bone of my bones, and flesh of my flesh: she shall be called Woman, because she was taken out of Man.

24 Therefore shall a man leave his father and his mother, and shall cleave unto his wife: and they shall be one flesh.

25 And they were both naked, the man and his wife, and were not ashamed.

If the above is to be translated into a LILY WHITE CREATION, why not an interpretation for a BLACK THEOLOGY with its comparative...

BLACK IMAGE FOR BLACK PEOPLE?... [1]

I guess we can all reflect upon the great words of INFERIOR WISDOM the "Great White Father" passed on down to one of our illustrious "NEGRO/COLORED CLERGY-MEN" of Chicago, Illinois - the Reverend Dr. "J" [who heads a group that reacts equally as "NIGGARDLY" as he does] when he was quoted as having said early in 1974 C.E. at a BAPTIST CONVENTION he and his dominated for years:

"THE AFRO-HAIR STYLE IS AS UN-GODLY AS SIN ITSELF".

This NEGRO/COLORED/HONORARY WHITE-FIELD NIGGER-type of mentality made many of the "HOUSE NEGROES" of equal ignorance begin to attack those of us who find no disgrace in our natural hair with the most vicious diatribe; all in the "NAME OF GOD" of course! They had failed to take a concentrated look at the WOOLLY HAIR of the MOTHER from whence all of them and their minister came into this world; not the WIG-HEADED and HOT-COMBED FRIED-HEADED BLACK-PRETENDING HONORARY WHITE STRAIGHT HAIR WOMAN WHO SHOWS NO PRIDE IN HER BLACK AND MOST BEAUTIFUL AFRICAN PERSONALITY that they could not find on their own celebrated "MOTHER OF GOD" Michaelangelo, Mantegna, DePuci and other European artists painted for their HOLY FAMILY in their own "IMAGE." Yet, is it not strange, these

---

1. Even J. Cone's BLACK THEOLOGY failed to project a BLACK JESUS from Black Theologians.

"NEGRO WOMEN" turned MENTALLY WHITE are our MOTHERS, SISTERS, DAUGH-
TERS, WIVES, GIRLFRIENDS, AUNTS, COUSINS, etc.; yes, "SELF HATE"!

In this reflective value of the need for an "AFRICAN THEOLOGY" the "African
Church Fathers" such as TERTULLIAN, ST. CYPRIAN and ST. AUGUSTINE's works
should be reconsidered, the following being just a mere sample of them:

> ON CHRISTIAN DOCTRINE, HOLY CITY OF GOD, CONFESSION, by
> Augustine; HOMOGENES, by Tertullian; and THE CHURCH, by Cyprian;

etc. , etc., etc. These Africans, along with their "AFRO-HAIR" and so-called "NE-
GROID CHARACTERISTICS, " caused even the most racist Christian Church historian
C. P. Groves in his four volumes work- THE PLANTING OF CHRISTIANITY IN AFRI-
CA, page 59 to write the following with respect to themselves and many of their African
sisters who died as martyrs of the same RELIGION and GOD - Jesus "the Christ":

> A certain Namphamo, claimed as the first
> martyr, also came from Numidia, the name in
> this case being Punic. As from this point the
> story of the Church in Africa unfolds before
> us, we find a devotion under persecution not
> excelled elsewhere, and a fervent fidelity to
> the faith expressed in Puritan ideals that
> gave Montanism a second home in Africa. The
> names Tertullian, Cyprian and Augustine add
> an imperishable lustre to the history of the
> African Church.

Mrs. Stewart Erskine in her book - VANQUISHED CITIES OF NORTHERN AFRICA,
page 80 tells the story of our African spiritual leaders in the following manner:

> The three great names that bring honour to the
> African Church are Tertullian, the first of the
> Church writers who made Latin the Language of
> Christianity; Cyprian, bishop and martyr; and
> Augustine, one of the most famous of the "Fathers
> of the Church.

The tone of the BLACK THEOLOGY I am advocating was set all the way back in the
earliest Christian period by Tertullian, the native of Khart-Haddas [Carthage] who
was born in ca. 155 C.E., when he wrote the following in De ANIMA, XXX [as quoted
in English by Harmack's MISSION AND EXPANSION, Vol. III, p. 275]:

> Surely a glance at the wide world shows that
> it is daily being more cultivated and better
> peopled than before. All places are now accessible,
> well known, open to commerce. Delightful farms have
> now blotted out every trace of the dreadful wastes;
> cultivated fields have overcome woods; flocks and
> herds have driven out wild beasts; sandy spots are
> sown, rocks are planted; bogs are drained. Large
> cities now occupy land hardly tenanted before by
> cottages. Islands are no longer dreaded; houses,
> people, civil rule, civilization, are everywhere.

6

Along with the reflection of the role Africans have played in the earliest form of CHRISTIANITY must be the role they played in changing the tone of CHRISTIANITY within the United States of America. For this we have to turn to the African [BLACK] Fathers of the BLACK CHRISTIAN CHURCH IN THE AMERICAS, such as the Rt. Rev. Bishop Richard Allen - founder of the AFRICAN METHODIST EPISCOPAL CHURCH [AME],Rev. William Palmer- founder of the AFRICAN BAPTIST CHURCH, and the Rev. Absolom Jones - founder of the AFRICAN PRESBYTERIAN CHURCH; all of this being the result of a WHITE [racist] CHRISTIAN THEOLOGY that denied them the freedom of RELIGIOUS DEVOTION in the CHRISTIAN RELIGION their indigenous African ancestors - PANTAEUS and BOETIUS- founded and developed in Ta-Merry [Egypt] and Ta-Nehisi [Sudan], which went farther south inItiopi [Ethiopia] and all over North Alkebu-lan [Africa] before it entered Greece and Rome in Europe.

Is this reflective of the thought behind the late Honourable Sage and Prophet Marcus Moziah Garvey's founding of the AFRICAN ORTHODOX CHURCH with its own BLACK HOLY FAMILY patterned after the ETHIOPIAN ORTHODOX [formerly Coptic] CHURCH for the Universal Negro Improvement Association and African Communities League, Inc. [UNIA]? Probably a quick glance at the pictures on pages 67-81 will help!

Is it reflective of the ideology of the late Prophet Elijah Mohammad [Poole] when he founded the NATION OF ISLAM [commonly "BLACK MUSLIM RELIGION" and/or "WAY OF LIFE [1] to help find a way out of the WHITE DEATH and other WHITE PLAGUES threatening to snuff out the lives of all humanity; which his sons now decry?

Is it reflective of the PHILOSOPHICAL CONCEPT outlined by the noted Mwalimu Jaramogi Agyeman [Rev. Albert A. Cleage, Jr.] when he began his BLACK CHRISTIAN NATIONALIST MOVEMENT [BCN] and established the various SHRINES OF THE BLACK MADONNA in Detroit, Mich.; Philadelphia, Pa.; Atlanta, Ga.; etc.?

Is it reflective of the depth of AFRICAN DIVINE SPIRITUALITY in the thoughts of the formerly incarcerated Teacher Ron Karenga [Everett] when he established his "SEVEN PRINCIPLES OF KAWAIDA" and the "KWANZA SPIRITUAL CEREMONY" that fall equally on the days when our ancient ancestors celebrated the EPHERIAL EQUI-NOX, which the European plagiarized and distorted to make their "CHRISTMAS"?

Is it reflective of all of the other DIVINE BLACK EXPRESSIONS I have not listed here; ail of which our BLACK THEOLOGIANS, even like Dr. James Cone in his work - BLACK THEOLOGY [New York, 1965], tried to express for a LILY WHITE academia

1. They overlooked Arab Muslim slavers who carried off Africans into slavery in Mecca and Medina, along with maintainance in Africa.

7

in terms WHITE AMERICA could not hold to be socio-politically offensive and/or truly sacriligious like the following from E. F. Frazier, THE NEGRO CHURCH IN AMERICA [New York, 1964], pages 6 - 8:

The Christian Religion Provides a New Basis of Social Cohesion

It is our position that it was not what remained of African culture or African religious experience but the Christian religion that provided the new basis of social cohesion. It follows then that in order to understand the religion of the slaves, one must study the influence of Christianity in creating solidarity among a people who lacked social cohesion and a structured social life.

From the beginning of the importation of slaves into the colonies, Negroes received Christian baptism. The initial opposition to the christening of Negroes gradually disappeared when laws made it clear that slaves did not become free through the acceptance of the Christian faith and baptism.[13] Although slaves were regularly baptized and taken into the Anglican church during the seventeenth century, it was not until the opening of the eighteenth century that a systematic attempt was made on the part of the Church of England to Christianize Negroes in America. This missionary effort was carried out by the Society for the Propagation of the Gospel in Foreign Parts which was chartered in England in 1701.[14] When the Indians in South Carolina proved to be so hostile to the first missionary sent out by the Society, he turned his attention to Negro and Indian slaves.

Unfortunately, we do not possess very detailed records on the religious behaviour of the Negroes who became converts to Christianity through the missionary efforts of the Society,[15] nor did the missionaries who worked under the auspices of the Moravians, Quakers, Presbyterians, and Catholics leave illuminating accounts of the response of the Negro slaves to their efforts. We do not know, for example, to what extent the converted slaves resumed their old 'heathen' ways or combined the new religious practices and beliefs with the old. In this connection it should be noted that the missionaries recognized the difficulty of converting the adult Africans and concentrated their efforts on the children.[16] However, there is no evidence that there was the type of syncretism or fusion of Christian beliefs and practices with African religious ideas and rituals such as one finds in the Candomblé in Brazil.[17] Despite the reported success in the conversion of Negroes, a study of the situation has revealed that only a small proportion of the slaves in the American colonies could be included among even nominal Christians.[18] In fact, the activities of the Anglican missionaries were directed to individuals whose isolation in the great body of slaves was increased.

As Woodson, the Negro historian, has so aptly called it, 'The Dawn of the New Day' in the religious development of Negroes occurred when the Methodists and Baptists began proselyting he blacks.[19]

"The Dawn Of The New Day", quoting Woodson through Frazier, was equally "The Dawn" Of A New Form Of Slavery - MENTAL and SPIRITUAL, each even worst than PHYSICAL SLAVERY imposed on AFRICAN/BLACK PEOPLE throughout the Americas.

8

The answer to all of these four questions is an emphatic ... "NO"...;with all of the energy and power one can summon from whatever SOURCE energy and power originated. Yes, from the same SOURCE "Black Power" is found.

"BLACK THEOLOGY", this ever-touching phrase of frightening dimension like its brother - "BLACK POWER" - and parents - "BLACK THOUGHT", has by itself ignited in AFRICAN PEOPLE the knowledge of their history and heritage. This is the so-called "... CARRY OVER..." Blacks had retained, but most of which has been beaten out of us before and after we set foot on the shores of the "Americas" and the Caribbean Islands from Alkebu-lan ["Africa, Afrika, Afrique", etc.]. Yet we must recapture all, and return them to the BLACK [African] SEMINARY in place of the LILY WHITE PHILOSOPHICAL and THEOSOPHICAL THOUGHTS that dominate each and everyone of the so-called "NEGRO/ COLORED SEMINARIES" existing today in each and every "NEGRO/COLORED INSTITU- TION OF HIGHER LEARNING" [institutes, colleges and universities, etc. - both private and paraochial].

The devouring question must naturally come forth:

'WHO WILL LEAD US BACK INTO BLACK THEOLOGY'?[1].

And naturally the "FEAR SYNDROME" must hit each and every existing "NEGRO" and/or "COLORED" theologian who has never before written the first word on any kind of a "THE- OLOGY" - Black or White - other than the half-baked regurgitation in his or her thesis or disertation for an undergraduate or postgraduate degree based upon "LILY WHITE THE- OLOGY" which I am questioning in this work. But it is they who must be FORCED by the BLACK, YOUNG and BEAUTIFUL SEMINARIANS and PARISHONERS - their PARENTS, GUARDIANS and WELL WISHERS - who are taxed with the task of the RE-AFRICANIZATION of our AFRICAN [Black if you prefer] INSTITUTIONS of a RELIGIOUS and/or SECULAR posture. For it is WE, ourselves, who must be willing to remove anyone of OUR current "NEGRO/COLORED THEOLOGIANS". They cannot repair and reconvert back to their form- er AFRICANESS or BLACKNESS in which they were originally CONCEIVED, NURTURED, BIRTHED, DEVELOPED and RAISED before their CORRUPTION due to the WHITENING PROCESS they received from their "BRAINWASHED" Board Of Trustees, Administrators and Faculty - all combined into the so-called "COLLEGE SENATE", etc.

What kind of INFORMATION, DOCUMENTS, ARTIFACTS, GODS, GODESSES, COM- MANDMENTS, ORIGIN OF OUR BLACK WORLD, MONOTHEISM, etc., etc., etc. are you

---

1. This "Black Theology" must reflect teachings from the world's very first Holy Scriptures [Bible] ever produced by human beings... The Egyptian Book Of The Dead and Papyrus of Ani.

suggesting my dear fellow is always the cry; as if those who are in control of WHITE
THEOLOGY in BLACK [Negro/Colored in fact] SEMINARIES do not truly have any idea
about these TRUTHS from our ancient fathers and mothers of Alkebu-lan who built the
following shrines, pyramids and temples to OUR BLACK GODS OF ALKEBU-LAN and
preached about in their BLACK THEOLOGY thousands of years before the myths and
allegories about an "ADAM AND EVE IN THE GARDEN OF EDEN" became the foundation story of what was to be later called "JUDAISM, CHRISTIANITY" and "ISLAM"!

The Sphinx of Gizeh as it appeared to Baron Denon in 1798 C.E., from one
of his own drawings he made first hand. Note the relative indigenous African
characteristics - nose, lips, etc. This was the way it appeared before Napoleon's
soldiers blew its face assunder in distaste of its "Negroid looks."This took
place during France's invasion of Egypt.
note: Why was this picture witheld from students and the general public?

CEMETERY PYRAMIDS and CANDACES
of Meröe and Ta-Nehisi

[Photo: Museum of Fine Arts, Boston, Mass.]

Foreground: SOUTHERN MECROPOLIS - IIIrd Century B.C.E.
Background: NORTHERN MECROPOLIS - IVth Century B.C.E. to C.E.

COLOSSAL Step Pyramid of Sakhara,   MEDIUM Pyramid of Ghiza, by Pharaoh
by Pharaoh Djoser, IIIrd Dynasty;   Snefru, IVth Dynasty.
architect and builder Imhotep.

10

GOD HARMACHIS: A SOURCE OF BLACK
THEOLOGY BEFORE GOD YWH/JEHOVAH, GOD JESUS, AND/OR GOD AL'LAH

The Sphinx of Gizeh as it appeared to Baron Denon in 1798 C.E., from one of his own drawings he made first hand. Note the relative indigenous African characteristics - nose, lips, etc. This was the way it appeared before Napoleon's soldiers blew its face assunder in distaste of its "Negroid looks."This took place during France's invasion of Egypt.

Note: Why was this picture witheld from students and the general public?

Akhet Khufu
[Horizon of Khufu]

The Sphinx as it appears in 1970; showing the temple and dream-stele.

HE WHO CONTROLS MY MIND CONTROLS
MY ENTIRE LIFE, SAYETH THE GODS
AND GODDESSES OF ALKEBU-LAN. [From
Y.A.A. ben-Jochannan's "Message Of My
Own Reconversion Back To My African Self-
Consciousness", 20 page paper written in
1939 C.E./A.D., San Juan, Puerto Rico]

Note: This is the grandeur of the so-called "BLACK AFRICANS" which brought about the racist attempt to remove any trace of the history of their presence all over North Africa and East Africa.
The gigantic architecture, the emmence engineering fete, the spiritual depth, etc., etc., etc. it
took to produce this creation startled the "Greek"students they brought from Europe to see such
as this. This was the beginning of a "civilizing process" of Europeans which unfortunately was ended when the students overpowered their teachers, thus leaving Europeans and European-Americans
to develop a "WHITE THEOLOGY MINUS A GOD OF COMPASSION" other than one who only acts on
Sundays and Saturdays to suit the collection plates. The saddest aspect of all of this is that BLACKS
have equally succumb to this irreligious religion of European Judaeo-Christianity.

11

"GREAT PYRAMIDS OF GHIZEH"
(Akhet Khufu, Horizon of Pharaoh Khufu)

(A view from the South)
Left: Pyramid of Khufu ("Cheops"), 147m high; Center: Pyramid of Khafra (Cheph-
ren), 143m high; Right: Men-kau-Ra ("Mycerinus"), 66.40m high. The three (3)
small Pyramids in the foreground are of Queens of the IVth Dynasty - c.? - 2258
B.C.E. [Encyclopedia of Egyptian Civilization, p. 195].
DIMENSIONS FOR PYRAMID OF KHUFU
L = 756'0" x W = 760'0" x H = 481'0". Angle created from base to extreme top:
51° 50'. Total mass: 3,277,000 Cubic Feet .

THE FOUR MOST GLORIOUS PHAROAHS AND PYRAMID BUILDERS
of the
"GREAT PYRAMID AGE"
(IIIrd through Vth Dynasty, c. 2780-2420 BCE)

Pharaoh Djoser, IIIrd Dynasty,
c.2780 - 2680. The STEP
PYRAMID OF SAKHARA . First
of the COLOSSAL PYRAMIDS.

Pharaoh Khufu, IVth Dynasty,
c. 2680 -2258, PYRAMID OF
GHIZA (147m high).

Pharaoh Khafra, IVth Dynasty,
c. 2680 - 2258, PYRAMID OF
GHIZA (143m high). Last of the
COLOSSAL PYRAMID builders .

Pharaoh Men-kau-Ra, IVth
Dynasty, c. 2780 - 2258,
PYRAMID OF GHIZA (66.40m
high). First of the MODERATE
PYRAMIDS.

BLACK SKIN, THICK LIPS, BROAD NOSE, AFRO-HAIR; JUST LIKE REV. JACKSON

Note: For further details see pages 10 - 14, Y. ben-Jochannan, BLACK MAN OF THE
NILE AND HIS FAMILY, New York, 1972.

12

BUILT BEFORE "ADAM AND EVE IN THE GARDEN OF EDEN" WERE CREATED

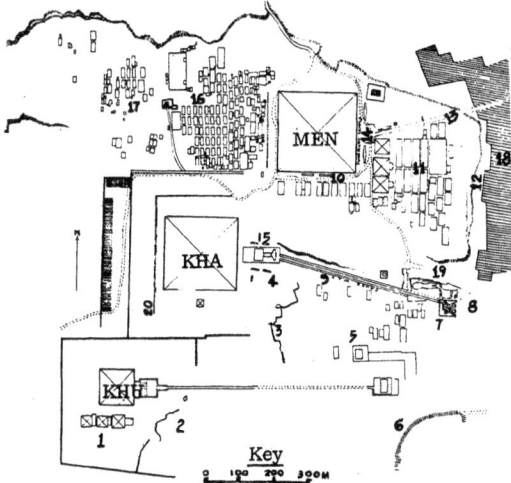

GENERAL AREA SITE PLAN OF THE PYRAMID FIELD
OF GHIZEH *

1. Funerary Temple	8. Temple of Great Sphinx	14. Funerary Temple
2. Men-kau-Rè Quarry	9. Cause Way	15. Funerary Temple of Khaf-Ra
3. Rock-cut Tombs	10. Boat Pitt of Khu-fu	16. Western Cemetery
4. Boat Pitts	11. Eastern Cemetery	17. Office of Pyramid Studies
5. Tomb of Khemt-ka-wes	12. Rock-cut Tombs	18. Village
6. Valley Temple of Men-kau-Rè	13. Cause Way	20. Rock-cut Tombs

KHU - Khufu, KHA - Knafra, MEN - Men-kau-Ra

---

*Like most of the archaeological sites of the Nile Valleys (Blue and White),
there are many ways to spell the names of different ones. The correct spelling
of this shrine is as shown above, but the following is also a most common way
in which it is also written - "GIZA." You will also note that many of the pharaohs (kings) names are written in different manners than you may be accoustomed
to seeing.

JUST IMAGINE!
NOT A SINGLE "HARIBU/ISRAELITE" OR "JEW" WAS YET CONCEIVED TO DATE
The Period - ca. 2180 - 2238 B.C.E. or B.C.

THE GREAT PYRAMIDS OF GHIZEH/HORIZON OF PHARAOH KHUFU, KHAFRA AND MEN-KAU-RA

Note: See Key on page 13 , sizes on page 13. The above is a view from south to north. The order of the pyramids from left to right: Khufu, Khafra and Men-kau-Ra. See following for individual pharaoh's pyramid.

14

THE FUNERARY TEMPLE OF PHARAOH MEN-KAU-RA AND PYRAMID OF PHARAOH KHAFRA

Note: Pyramid of Pharaoh Khafra is in the background, Temple in foreground.

THE SPHINX AND VALLEY TEMPLE OF PHARAOH KHAFRA

Sphinx at front-left, pyramid in left background, and temple in foreground.

Note: This entire complex was built before the birth of the very first Haribu/Hebrew/Jew, etc. named Abraham. Thus it preceded the OLD TESTAMENT/PENTATEUCH/HOLY TORAH/FIVE BOOKS OF MOSES, even the Judaeo–Christian gods – YWH/JEHOVAH and JESUS ["the Christ"], and of course the Moslem god AL'LAH....Amen–Ra.

THE FOURTH DYNASTY'S [ca. 2680 – 2565 B. C. E.] DASHUR PYRAMIDS AND SAND DOOMS

STEP PYRAMID OF PHARAOH DJOSER/SER
DESIGNED AND BUILT BY A "BLACK MAN" FOR HIS "BLACK GOD" BEFORE "YWH MADE MAN IN THE GARDEN OF EDEN" FOR THE HARIBU ["Jews"]

Reconstruction of funerary buildings by Jean-Philippe Lauer, Paris, France. Main PYRAMID dimensions: L=431'0" x W= 344'0" x H=200'0". Height of exterior wall enclosure, 33'0".

Southern Elevation of the Step Pyramid of Sakhara (Saqqara)

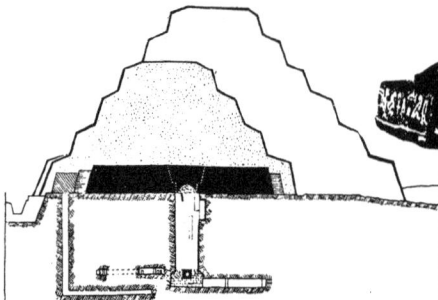

Cross Section of Step Pyramid [Cut West-East]
View South to North

IMHOTEP
Architect and builder for Djoser [Ser], 3rd Pharaoh of the IIIrd Dynasty, ca. 2780 - 2680 B.C.E.; also Physician Poet, Philosopher, Astronomer, Grand Vizier and Author

LARGER AND HIGHER THAN THE "TOWER OF BABEL"

THE TEMPLE/TOMB OF PHARAOH DJOSER [Foreground] AND STEP PYRAMID OF GHIZEH/GIZA

Conceived, designed, planned and constructed by Architect Imhotep

Note: Djoser, whom Herodotus renamed Zoser, was also known as "Ser" in ancient Nile Valley High-Cultures.

PORTICO OF THE "HALL OF PILLARS" OF THE TEMPLE/TOMB OF PHARAOH
DJOSER/SER, 3rd PHARAOH of IIIrd DYNASTY

Note: In the extreme rear a semblance of the Step Pyramid is visible.

THEY WERE BUILT TO SUIT A "BLACK THEOLOGY" FOR A "BLACK GOD"

Some antiquities of Zimbabwe

A photographic view (from the north-east) of the ruins of Queen Hatshepsut s Funerary at Luxor [Thebes] or Deir el-Bahri

(1) Vulture's head; (2) Model of ruins; (3) Oxen; (4) Head of man
(5) Hunt (the hunter is shown as suffering from steatopygia)

(6) Round, massive tower

Pharaoh
Ra-mer-ka Amen-tarit
ca. 100 B.C.E.
Nubian

Pharaoh Tek – Amen
ca. 30 B.C.E.
Nubian

RUINS OF THE TEMPLE OF THE STEP PYRAMID
OF SAKHARA

22

TEMPLE/TOMB OF QUEEN-PHARAOH HATSHEPSUT AT THEBES

Also Known As "Der-el-Bahri/Thebes"

UPPER COURT OF THE TEMPLE/TOMB OF QUEEN-PHARAOH
HATSHEPSUT, AT THEBES

Note: The only woman in recorded history to rule simultaneously as Queen and Pharaoh [King] of a country, Egypt; thus calling herself "Queen-Pharaoh/King. She was the daughter Pharaoh Thutmoses I.

AFRICAN "MORAL LAWS" OF GOD:

The HUMANITY within the BLACK THEOLOGY that built the temples, pyramids and other structures we have just reviewed has been to some extent carried to the so-called "NEW WORLD"[or "WESTERN HEMISPHERE" and "AMERICAS"]by the ancestors of those who now choose to call themselves by the ridiculous nomenclatures...

"NEGROES, COLOREDS, NIGGERS",

etc., etc., etc.; as they equally hold contempt for anyone and anything that suggests their total...

ALKEBU-LAN ["African"] ORIGIN....

This is so because they are not aware that:

Ist:
We must go back to the oldest sources of written records existing to date; thus all of the archives, libraries and museums [public and private] where the Nile Valley and Great Lakes African People's works are kept by the European, European-American and Asian thieves and receivers of STOLEN LEGACY from "Africa," such as the BOOK OF THE DEAD and PAPYRUS ANI, PYRAMID TEXTS, COFFIN TEXTS, TEACHINGS OF PHARAOH AMEN-EM-EOPE, PAPYRUS OF SET, etc.

IInd:
We must examine the oldest written document existing on religion I have mentioned above - THE BOOK OF THE COMING FORTH BY DAY AND BY NIGHT [or Book Of The Dead and Papyrus Of Ani] to compare it with the adoptions made in the Judaeo-Christian-Islamic BIBLES - Pentateuch [Old Testament], Koiñe Bible [New Testament] and Holy Qur'an [Koran],and read them in their original languages before the major VERSIONS carried their total distortions.

IIIrd:
We must examine the source of the "LAWS" that were given the name "COMMANDMENTS" and see why they regulated our ancient values of MORALITY, ETHICAL CULTURE, SOCIO-POLITICAL BEHAVIOR and ECONOMIC salvation in our High-Cultures [civilizations]; then look what has happened, what should happen, and why. This would require that we look into the so-called "NEGATIVE CONFESSIONS" - at least 147 responses to as many "COMMANDMENTS, including the so-called TEN COMMANDMENTS certain "Jewish" falsifiers and their scribes still attribute to a later origin by a fellow African named "MOSES,"which we can read about in the much later religion called "JUDAISM" and its "STOLEN LEGACY" about the so-called "CREATION OF MAN, RECEIVING OF THE LAWS, ATONEMENT, NETHER or NEXT WORLD and also HEREAFTER, etc.; a sample of each I am showing from pages 138 and 139 of my AFRICAN ORIGINS OF THE MAJOR WESTERN RELIGIONS - JUDAISM, CHRISTIANITY, ISLAM, ETC.:

The concept of the making of man (creation) by

"ONE" - the Sun-God RA, who was sometimes identified with the God OSIRIS, was in fact dealing with a monotheistic God even though polytheism seemed to be the basic foundation of the African religions of Sais (later called "EGYPT" by the Hebrews, Greeks and Romans). Yet one sees, in the BOOK OF THE DEAD - as translated from Hieroglyph to English by Sir E. A. Wallis-Budge, Chapter clxxxii, 1.15, Osiris shown as the only God who could make man inherit "everlasting and eternal life;" also that he alone had the power to :

> "... cause men and women to be born again...."

The same God, OSIRIS, was responsible to represent "ONE" - the "SUPREME BEING," as He "...loved life and hated death...;" this having been shown in the following extract from Chapter cliv of the BOOK OF THE DEAD:

> "...Homage to thee, O my divine father Osiris,
> thou hast thy being with thy members. Thou didst
> not decay, thou didst not turn into worms, thou
> didst not rot away, thou didst not become cor-
> ruption, thou didst not putrefy.... I shall not
> decay, I shall not rot, I shall not putrefy....
> I shall have my being, I shall live, I shall
> germinate, I shall wake up in peace.... My body
> shall be established, and it shall neither fall
> into ruin nor be destroyed off this earth.

The above prayer was by Pharoah Thotmes III (1550 - 1504 B.C E.) to the God Osiris. One can see the basic values of death and its treatment from this episode and its corruption in the Hebrew which followed many hundreds of years later.

The teachings about "LIFE, DEATH, RESURRECTION, HEREAFTER," etc. above are followed by teachings and sayings that European and European-American "egyptologists" and "philosophers" in their "stolen legacy" from our ancestors High-Cultures "NEGATIVE CONFESSIONS"[1] - 42 of the total 147:

1) I have not done iniquity.
2) I have not committed robbery with violence.
3) I have done violence to no man.
4) I have not committed theft.
5) I have not slain man or woman.
6) I have not made light the bushel.
7) I have not acted deceitfully.
3) I have not purloined the things which belonged to the God.

9) I have not uttered falsehood.
10) I have not carried away food.
11) I have not uttered evil words.
12) I have not attacked man.
13) I have not killed the beasts which are the property of the Gods.
14) I have not eaten my heart (i.e., done anything to my regret).
15) I have not laid waste ploughed land.
16) I have never pried into matters.
17) I have not set my mouth in motion against any man.
18) I have not given way to anger concerning myself without cause.
19) I have not defiled the wife of a man.
20) I have not committed transgression against any party.
21) I have not violated sacred times and seasons.
22) I have not struck fear into any man.
23) I have not been a man of anger.
24) I have not made myself deaf to words of right and truth.
25) I have not stirred up strife.
26) I have not made no man weep.
27) I have not committed acts of impurity or sodomy.
28) I have not eaten my heart.
29) I have not abused no man.
30) I have not acted with violence.
31) I have not judged hastily.
32) I have not taken vengeance upon the God.
33) I have not multiplied my speech overmuch.
34) I have not acted with deceit, or worked wickedness.
35) I have not cursed the king.
36) I have not fouled water.
37) I have not made haughty my voice.
38) I have not cursed the God.
39) I have not behaved with insolence.
40) I have not sought for distinctions.
41) I have not increased my wealth except with such things as are my own possessions.
42) I have not thought scorn of the God who is in the city.

IVth:

We must look at those works which detail the contents of the BOOK OF THE DEAD, such as teachings in the PYRAMID TEXTS [writings on the walls of pyramids, papyrae and artifacts found therein] and COFFIN TEXTS [writings taken from the outside and inside of the casket which houses the mummified remains of the deceased like the Scribe Ani], and as demonstrated below:

We do not need any more proof of this than the following from "The Doctrine Of Eternal Life" found in the PYRAMID TEXT,[1] which preceded the OLD TESTAMENT by thousands of years.

| Rise up thou | Teta | this. | Stand up thou | mighty one |

| being strong. | Sit thou | with the gods, | do thou | that which |

---

1. Do not loose sight of the fact that these Sacred Scriptures can be purchased in English translation.

did   Osiris in the great house in Ånu. Thou hast received

thy *såh*, not   shall be fettered thy foot in heaven, not

shalt thou be turned back upon earth.

2. Hail to thee, Tetá on   this thy day [when] thou art

standing before Rå [as] he cometh from the east, [when] thou art

endued with   this thy *såh*   among   the souls.

3. [His] duration of life is eternity, his limit of life is everlastingness

in   his *såh*.

4. I am   a *såh* with his soul.

Vth:

We must reexamine the TEACHINGS OF PHARAOH AMEN-EM-EOPE
that preceded the "PROVERBS" that were attributed to a Hebrew King
by the name of "SOLOMON" and compare them to   their true
origin;and also who was the thief of this STOLEN LEGACY, as shown
below from pages 164 and 165 of AFRICAN ORIGINS OF THE "WEST-
ERN RELIGIONS: JUDAISM, CHRISTIANITY, ISLAM, ETC.:

THE COMPARATIVE WORKS [1]

The Teachings of Amen-em-ope Pharoah of Egypt (1405-1370)	The so-called "Proverbs" of King Solomon of Israel (976-936)
Give thine ear, and hear what I say, And apply thine heart to apprehend;	Incline thine ear, and hear my words, And apply thine heart to apprehend;
It is good for thee to place them in thine heart, Let the rest in the cas- ket of the belly. That they may act as a peg upon thy tongue. •••••	For it is pleasant if thou keep them in thy belly, That they may be fixed upon thy lips. •••••
Consider these thirty chapters; They delight, they in- struct. Knowledge how to answer him that speaketh, And how to carry back a	Have I not written for thee thirty sayings, Of counsels and knowledge! That thou mayest make known truth to him that speaketh.

---

1. It is extremely important that this, and other such works, become part of your own library.

report to one that sent it. • • • • • Beware of robbing the poor, And of oppressing the afflicted. • • • • • Associate not with a passionate man, Nor approach him for conversations; Leap not to cleave to such a one, That the terror carry thee not away. • • • • • A scribe who is skillful in his business Findeth himself worthy to be a courtier. • • • • •	• • • • • Rob not the poor for he is poor, Neither oppress the lowly in the gate. • • • • • Associate not with a passionate man, Nor go with a wrathful man, Lest thou learn his ways, And get a snare to thy soul. • • • • • A man who is skillful in his in his business Shall stand before kings. • • • • •

The plagiarism on <u>Solomon's</u> part cannot be overlooked; as he too often copied <u>Amen-em-ope's</u> work in too many instances word for word. For added comparisons one only needs to secure books on this subject listed in the bibliography of this work.[1]

6th:

We must go back into our past and look for the origin of the theory about "MONOTHEISM" which certain Jewish scribes who wrote the PENTA-TEUCH [<u>Old Testament</u> or <u>Five Books Of Moses</u>] attributed to the African named "MOSES," instead of its true African authority - Pharaoh Amenhotep IVth, who was also known as "AKHENATEN, IKHNATON," etc. He was the PROPHET, TEACHER, SCRIBE, ELECT OF GOD, PRINCE OF PEACE, etc. who wrote the following about the "<u>One And Only True God</u> - ATEN...

father in the beginning," ⟨hieroglyphs⟩; "the Maker of
" things which are. Creator of things which shall be. Source
" of the lands, Father of fathers, Mother of mothers,"
⟨hieroglyphs⟩;
" Father of the fathers of the gods and goddesses, lord of
" things created in himself, maker of heaven, and earth, and
" the Tuat, and water, and the mountains," ⟨hieroglyphs⟩
⟨hieroglyphs⟩; "supporter of the sky upon
its four pillars, raised up of the same in the firmament (?) "
⟨hieroglyphs⟩...

This has been plagiarized in the so-called FIVE BOOKS OF MOSES to

---

1. African sources in this "bibliography" must become teaching aides in your religious institution.

read as follows in GENESIS Chapter i, Verses 1 - 5:

PHARAOH AKHENATEN and FAMILY

ca. 1370 - 1352 B.C.E. ???
XVIIIth Dynasty

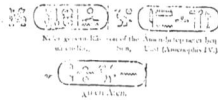

Pharaoh Amen-ophis III,
father of
Pharaoh Akhenaten
ca. 1405 - 1370 B.C.E. ???
XVIIIth Dynasty

daughter of
Pharaoh Akhenaten
[Wife of Pharaoh
Tut-ankh-Anon
1352 - 1350 BCE]

Queen Tiyi
mother of
Pharaoh Akhenaten

Queen Nefertiti
wife of
Pharaoh Akhenaten
[Amen-hotep   IV]

7th:

We must reexamine the GEOGRAPHICAL AREA of the so-called
"Garden Of Eden" and its rivers - "PISON, GIHON" and "HID-
DEKEL" - and the LAND over which the GREAT DELUGE [flood]
took place according to GENESIS Chapter vii, Verses 17 - 24, and

30

THE WORLD OF GENESIS
ca. 1675 BCE

8 And God called the firmament Heaven. And the evening and the morning were the second day.

of the earth separated from the waters,

9 ¶ And God said, Let the waters under the heaven be gathered together unto one place, and let the dry *land* appear: and it was so.

10 And God called the dry *land* Earth; and the gathering together of the waters called he Seas: and God saw that *it was* good.

and made fruitful,

11 And God said, Let the earth bring forth grass, the herb yielding seed, *and* the fruit tree yielding fruit after his kind, whose seed *is* in itself, upon the earth: and it was so.

12 And the earth brought forth grass, *and* herb yielding seed after his kind, *and* the tree yielding fruit, whose seed *was* in itself, after his kind: and God saw that *it was* good.

13 And the evening and the morning were the third day.

of the sun, moon and stars,

14 ¶ And God said, Let there be lights in the firmament of the heaven to divide the day from the night;

and let them be for signs, and for seasons, and for days, and years:

15 And let them be for lights in the firmament of the heaven to give light upon the earth: and it was so.

16 And God made two great lights; the greater light to rule the day, and the lesser light to rule the night: *he made* the stars also.

Thus we also look as the peoples who inhabited the LAND OF CANAAN and all of the other LANDS over which the THREE RIVERS flowed or supplied with water for the flourishing of its crops, and watering of its animals, also transportation of its peoples, etc. I have shown many of these people on pages 32 - 38 following. We must remember that these are the same so-called "SEMITES, HAMITES, NEGROIDS", etc. our European and European-American WHITE racists and religious bigots that dominate our education told us were "CAUCASIANS" in each and every institution of higher education throughout the United States of America.

31

NILE VALLEYS AFRICANS; NOT ONE A "NEGRO"

KEY

1. Ta-Nehisi (Nubia)	5. Ta-Merry (Kimit)
2. Ta-Merry (Egypt)	6. Ta-Nehisi (Nubia)
3. Itiopi (Ethiopia)	7. Bunyoro (Uganda)
4. Ta-Nehisi (Meroe)	8. Puanit (Kenya, etc.)

Any of the above indigenous Africans of centuries ago and the present can be seen by the millions all over the continent of Alkebu-lan, "MOTHER AFRICA".

Manqbetou   CongoQueen

The queen at the left is the only "NEGRO" on this page, according to "White Academia. The princess on the right is a different race called HAMITE according to THE SPHERE, February 13, 1937. She is the sister of the late King [Mwani]of Ruanda, Central Africa which is directly connected to the ITURI FOREST REGION where the TWA/HUTU live.

WHEN THE AFRICANS ["Blacks"] WERE THE "GODS" OF THE WORLD

The scene above is from a painting in TOMB 63 of Ta-Merry (Egypt). Like many others on the wall, it shows Assyrian (Syrian) subjects and tribute-bearers bringing quiver, vessels, ointment, and other material goods for the African Pharaoh. Note one of the gifts is a little child; probably a "SEMITE!"

The wall-painting above would be designated one of 'NEGRO SLAVES FROM NUBIA PAYING TRIBUTE TO THEIR EGYPTIAN RULER' if the people were Nubians. Since the people are designated "SEMITIC," the nomenclature - "SLAVES" - does not apply. Why is this so? The answer, RACISM and RELIGIOUS BIGOTRY.

THEIR "SEMITIC GOD" WAS SUBJECT TO THE "NEGRO GOD;" THEY HAD TO ADOPT A "BLACK THEOLOGY"

KA-APER, so-called "SHEIKH-el-BELED"

Note: Renamed "Sheikh-el-Beled" by the Arab Moslem invaders of Egypt in 640 C.E./A.D.

THICK LIPS, BROAD NOSE, BLACK COLOR AND "AFRICAN"
AGAINST THEIR "SEMITIC" RELATIVE

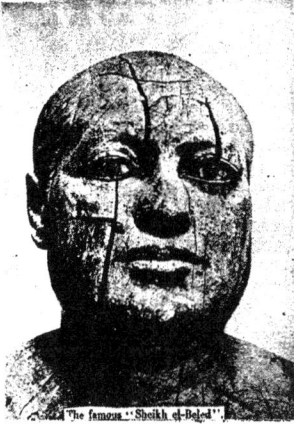

The famous "Sheikh el-Beled".

The term "Sheik [el-Beled"] is from the
Arabic language meaning "MAYOR".

Note cracks developed in the wood statue over the years

ORIENTAL INSTITUTE, UNIVERSITY OF CHICAGO

Ra-hotep and Nofert.

IVth Dynasty Pharaoh and Queen

Ta-Nehisian [Nubian, Zetis or Sudanese] and Assyrian KINGS paying
homage to Queen-Pharaoh Hatshepsut during the XVIIIth Dynasty - ca.
1515 - 1488 B.C.E. A very common scene in Ta-Merry [Egypt, Sais]

TYPICAL "SEMITES" AND "HAMITES"
OF BIBLICAL TIMES
THICK LIPS, BROAD NOSE, WOOLLY HAIR, AND BLACK/BURNT SKIN

Right: A "TYPICAL" African of
the type commonly found all
along the Nile Valley (Blue and
White) to the present day, 1972.
Left: Pharaoh Neb-Maat-Ra,
mighty ruler and builder of the
the 17th Pyramid.

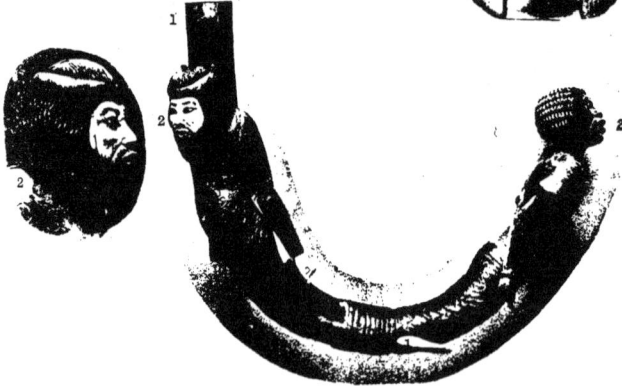

Handle of Pharaoh Tut-ankh-Amon's WALKING STICK

1 Ceremonial staff or Walking Stick with curved end (turned upside-down) used
by Pharaoh Tut-ankh-Amen of the XVIIIth Dynasty, c. ? - 1349 B.C.E., in official state functions. On the left of the curve is a "...BEARDED SEMITE...; at
the right a "...NEGRO." Note that these men were both "...PRISONERS." The
insert at the extreme left is an enlarged image of the profile of the "SEMITE" or
"SYRIAN PRISONER;" the "NEGRO" or "NUBIAN PRISONER" is at the right. The
Walking Stick was stolen from the tomb of Pharaoh Tut-ankh-Amen and kept in
the Cairo Museum, Cairo , Egypt (Ta-Merry, Alkebu-lan or Africa).
2.   The same comparison made between the "SEMITE" and the "NEGRO" above
is also applicable to all of the Pharaohs of Ta-Merry prior to the arrival of the
so-called "HYKSOS SEMITES" from Asia around c. 1675 B.C.E. (Vth Dynasty);
this being equally true for the so-called "INDO-EUROPEAN ARAYANS" from Persia
in c. 525 B.C.E. (XXVIIth Dynasty), and the Macedonian-Greeks who followed
the Persians in c.332 B.C.E. (the so-called "XXXIIIrd Dynasty).

Note: Maybe our European and European-American CAUCASIAN/SEMITIC JEWS would prefer that
the above document did not exist! Probably the HASIDIC JEWS of Crown Heights, Brooklyn, New
York City, New York would realize from this that the above "BLACK SEMITES" represent part and
parcel of their own ORIGIN IN AFRICA by way of the AFRICAN NAMED MOSHE/MOSES. Thus their
own ANCESTRY RACIALLY/ETHNICALLY, of course including the mythical "JEWISH MOTHER",
came from the same source - ALEKBU-LAN/"AFRICA" - like the young AFRICAN/BLACK MAN
too many of their young and old goons/vigilantes tried to murder without any provocation by him.

36

We must look at the <u>Land</u> <u>Mass</u> [with the continents and peoples concerned] related to the EXODUS and/or PASSOVER led by "Moses" and the so-called "ISRAELITE PEOPLES" [there was no Israel during this period, ca. 1298 - 1232 B.C.E.] to see if they were different from those I have already shown in Moses' GENESIS story and the so-called "NEGROES/COLOREDS" of the United States of America, the rest of North America, South and Central America and the Caribbean Islands, also the so-called "PYGMIES, BANTUS" and "HOTTENTOTS" following the MAP OF THE WORLD OF EXODUS below:

THE WORLD OF EXODUS
ca. 1298 - 1232 BCE

Central Africans

"Bushman" M.L. King, Jr. R.E. Bunche "Mafutiminga Amooriape

WHITE THEOLOGY SAYS THEY ARE NOT RELATED, DOES BLACK THEOLOGY?

9th:

We must examine the writing in the PENTATEUCH [Five Books Of Moses, Holy Torah, Old Testament, Comesh, etc.] of an origin not older than 1078 years [ca. 700 B.C.E. - 1978 C.E.] that followed the BOOK OF THE COMING FORTH BY DAY AND BY NIGHT [or Egyptian Book Of The Dead and Papyrus Of Ani] which was already edited in ca. 4100 B.C.E., more than 6077 years ago, a period of 3400 years before the so-called "HOLY BIBLE." Some of its teachings follow below:

The physical body of man considered as a whole was called *khat* 𓂀𓃒𓏏𓏛, a word which seems to be connected with the idea of something which is liable to decay. The word is also applied to the mummified body in the tomb, as we know from the words "My body (*khat*) is buried." Such a body was attributed to the god Osiris; in the CLXIInd Chapter of the Book of the Dead "his great divine body rested in Anu." In this respect the god and the deceased were on an equality. As we have seen above, the body neither leaves the tomb nor reappears on earth; yet its preservation was necessary. Thus the

deceased addresses Temu : "Hail to thee, O my father "Osiris, I have come and I have embalmed this my flesh "so that my body may not decay. I am whole, even as "my father Kheperà was whole, who is to me the type of "that which passeth not away. Come then, O Form, and "give breath unto me, O lord of breath, O thou who art "greater than thy compeers. Stablish thou me, and form "thou me, O thou who art lord of the grave. Grant thou "to me to endure for ever, even as thou didst grant unto "thy father Temu to endure ; and his body neither passed "away nor decayed. I have not done that which is hateful "unto thee, nay, I have spoken that which thy KA loveth ; "repulse thou me not, and cast thou me not behind thee. "O Temu, to decay, even as thou doest unto every god and "unto every goddess and unto every beast and creeping "thing which perisheth when his soul hath gone forth from "him after his death, and which falleth in pieces after his 'decay . . . . . Homage to thee, O my father Osiris, thy "flesh suffered no decay, there were no worms in thee, "thou didst not crumble away, thou didst not wither away, "thou didst not become corruption and worms ; and I "myself am Kheperà, I shall possess my flesh for ever and "ever, I shall not decay, I shall not crumble away, I shall "not wither away, I shall not become corruption."

But the body does not lie in the tomb inoperative, for by the prayers and ceremonies on the day of burial it is endowed with the power of changing into a *sahu*, or spiritual body. Thus we have such phrases as, "I flourish (literally, ' 'sprout ') like the plants," "My flesh flourisheth," "I "exist. I exist, I live, I live, I flourish. I flourish,"

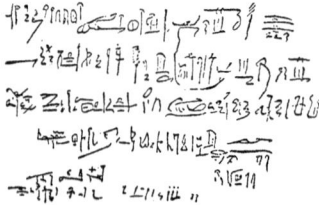

"...the son having... you have conquered the worlds at once Ammon Ra-Harmachis,"God of the first time, who alone

---

1. See statue that symbolizes God Ammon Ra-Harmachis on pp. 4, 10 and 11 of this volume.

gives life, health, and time of many praises to the groom
... of the Khen, son of the Royal son of Cush, Opener of
the road, Maker of transport boats, Giver of instructions
his lord...Amensha...."

This we have done, taking note of the fact that the plagiarizms in the so-called FIVE BOOKS OF MOSES are very clear in each and everyone of the stories we can identify with the teachings in the works of our indigenous African ancestors of the Nile Valley and Great Lakes High-Cultures. We should note that the name "CUSH/KUSH" appeared in our Egyptian works before the PENTATEUCH; equally the teaching related to "SON OF THE LORD" or "SON OF GOD," etc.

10th:
We must reexamine the NICENE CONFERENCE OF BISHOPS findings of ca. 322 - 325 C.E. to understand the THEORY and/or HYPOTHESIS of the "IMMACULATE CONCEPTION" and/or "VIRGIN BIRTH" and their relationship to the ISIS AND HORUS story that preceded them by more than 4422 years [ca. 4100 B.C.E. - 322 - 325 C.E.]; equally with respect to the "HOLY TRINITY" that Pharaoh Akhenaten taught to his fellow Africans of the Nile Valley more than 1666 years before the calling of the BISHOPS by Emperor Constantine["the great"] of Rome; also why they had maintained there was no SEXUAL INTERCOURSE in Mary's family for over three generations: Mary's MOTHER, Mary's GRAND-MOTHER, and Mary's own self, the latter teaching we find in the following from the LOST BOOKS OF THE BIBLE and FORGOTTEN BOOKS OF EDEN, all of which have been suppressed by those in-charge of Christian religious propaganda over the last 1650 years to date.

THE
Apocryphal New Testament.

The GOSPEL of the BIRTH OF MARY.

[In the primitive ages there was a Gospel extant bearing this name, attri-buted to St. Matthew, and received as genuine and authentic by several of the ancient Christian sects. It is to be found in the works of Jerome, a Father of the Church, who flourished in the fourth century, from whence the present translation is made. His contemporaries, Epipha-nius, Bishop of Salamis, and Austin, also mention a Gospel under this title. The ancient copies differed from Jerome's, for from one of them the learned Faustus, a native of Britain, who became Bishop of Riez, in Provence, endeavoured to prove that Christ was not the Son of God till after his baptism; and that he was not of the house of David and tribe of Judah, because, according to the Gospel he cited, the Virgin herself was not of this tribe, but of the tribe of Levi; her father being a priest of the name of Joachim. It was likewise from this Gospel that the sect of the Collyridians, established the worship and offering of man-chet bread and cracknels, or fine wafers, as sacrifices to Mary, whom they imagined to have been born of a Virgin, as Christ is related in the Canonical Gospel to have been born of her. Epiphanius likewise cites a passage concerning the death of Zacharias, which is not in Jerome's copy, viz. "That it was the occasion of the death of Zacharias in the temple, that when he had seen a vision, he, through surprise, was willing to disclose it, and his mouth was stopped. That which he saw was at the time of his offering incense, and it was a man standing in the form of an ass. When he was gone out, and had a mind to speak thus to the people, Woe unto you, whom do ye worship? he who had appeared to him in the temple took away the use of his speech. Afterwards when he recovered it, and was able to speak, he declared this to the Jews, and they slew him. They add (viz. the Gnostics in this book), that on this very account the high-priest was appointed by their lawgiver (by God to Moses), to carry little bells, that whensoever he went into the temple to sacrifice, he, whom they worshipped, hearing the noise of the bells, might have time enough to hide himself, and not be caught in that ugly shape and figure."—The principal part of this Gospel is con-tained in the Protevangelion of James, which follows next in order.]

1. See THE LOST BOOKS OF THE BIBLE AND THE FORGOTTEN BOOKS OF EDEN, p. 17

All of the data and artifacts [pictures, maps, graphs, etc.] I have shown thus far could be classified as The New "BLACK TEN COMMANDMENTS" for The New BLACK THEOLÓGY; that is if we [BLACK PEOPLE] are strong enough to act authoritatively in our OLD BLACK CHURCH and be "...born again..."[I Cor.].

What have we learned by these cherished "CARRY-OVERS" from our glorious RELIGIOUS HERITAGE that reaches back into the past more than 6233 years before the birth of the allegorical "ADAM AND EVE" of Genesis, Chapter ii, Verse 19 - where "...THE MAN..." God made or created first got his name; as all other references from Genesis, Chapter i, Verses 1 - 29 and Chapter ii, Verses 1 - 18 only refer to "God's' MALE CREATION" as "THE MAN" [a check of these two Chapters and Verses would be very helpful at this time]; all of this in the so-called "FIVE BOOKS OF MOSES" [not one of which Moses wrote before his death in ca. 1190 BCE] ?

Another question for all of us must now be:

HOW CAN THESE FACTS FIT INTO OUR BLACK THEOLOGY?

The AFRICAN [Black] THEOLOGY to which I am addressing my AFRICAN brothers and sisters is obvious in my presentations in some of the following works I have already published, such as:

> Black Man Of The Nile [Ist Edition 1970, to 5th impression], Alkebu-lan Books Associates,
> New York, N.Y., 1971
>
> African Origins Of The Major "Western Religions," [same publisher, 1970]
>
> Africa: Mother Of "Western Civilization" [same publisher, 1971]
>
> The Black Man's North And East Africa [same publisher, co-authors: Y. ben-Jochannan
> and G.E. Simmonds, 1971]
>
> Black Man Of The Nile And His Family [same publisher, 1972]
>
> Cultural Genocide In The Black And African Studies Curriculum [same publisher, 1973]
>
> A Chronology Of The Bible: Challenge To The Standard Version [same publisher, 1973]
>
> The Need For A Holy Black Bible, Vol. III [same publisher, 1974]
>
> Extracts and Comments From The Holy Black Bible [same publisher, 1974]

The following facts and details in the text of this work will supplement other factors we need to know in our "BLACK THEOLOGY, BLACK PHILOSOPHY, BLACK THEOSOPHY," etc.

The FIRST STEP will have to be a presentation of AFRICAN RELIGIONS, GODS and GODESSES [other than those already distorted in the Judaeo-Christian-Islamic mistique] and their THEOSOPHICAL theories which we tend to place under the White Racist Judaeo-Christian missionaries and anthropologists labels as "TRADITIONAL AFRICAN RELIGIONS" and "FETISHISMS." This we will have to do from writings and extracts by Africans who are of the various religions we are examining; not from racist and bigotted European and European-American WHITE and NEGRO missionaries whose sole reason for going to, or being in, Africa was, is and will always be to decry and destroy African Cultures [including our religious experiences], People and Religions.

The SECOND STEP will have to be a detailed analysis of the "SPIRIT WORLD" involved in our so-called "ANCESTRAL WORSHIP" which the Judaeo-Christian missionaries have DISTORTED to make their STOLEN LEGACY in religion appear to be that much more GODLY than others.

The THIRD STEP will have to be field trips to the actual land, and amongst the indigenous Africans of the specific religion and theology we are examining.

The FOURTH STEP will have to be the development of an archive of documents and other artifacts, besides and including visual and oral aids [video tapes and recorded tapes] to complement a library that reflects all of the works mentioned before and those to follow in the BIBLIOGRAPHY of this work; and yet more.

The FIFTH STEP will have to be guest lectures by the indigenous "AUTHORI - TIES" in each religion we examine, such as PRIESTS and PRIESTESSES, HERBAL- ISTS, METAPHYSICISTS and MENTAMPHYSICIANS, along with others [both male and female].

The SIXTH STEP is an honest analysis of all of the God-Heads with complement- ary allegories and mythologies sorrounding their creation and birth – like JESUS "the Christ" and the other "SIXTEEN CRUCIFIED SAVIORS" that preceded him.

The SEVENTH STEP must be research and writing cadres to analyze the avail- able materials and artifacts used in Judaeo-Christian and Islamic THEOSOPHY and THEOLOGY with respect to the PHILOSOPHICAL MYSTICISM the French Reverend Placide Temples even labeled "BANTU PHILOSOPHY" in his book of like name pub- lished in 1898 C.E., as shown in the following extract from pages 13 - 14:

IN SEARCH OF A BANTU PHILOSOPHY

1. Life and death determine human behaviour.

It has been often remarked that an European who has given up, during his life, all practice of the Christian religion, quickly returns to a Christian viewpoint when suffering or pain raise the problem of the preservation and survival or the loss and destruction of his being. Many sceptics turn, in their last moments, to seek in the ancient Christian teaching of the West, the practical answer to the problem of redemption or destruction. Suffering and death are ever the two great apostles who lead many wanderers in Europe at their last moments to our traditional Christian wisdom.

In the same way among our Bantu we see the évolués,[1] the "civilized", even the Christians, return to their former ways of behaviour whenever they are overtaken by moral lassitude, danger or suffering. They do so because their ancestors left them their practical solution of the great problem of humanity, the problem of life and death, of salvation or destruction. The Bantu, only converted or civilized superficially, return at the instance of a determining force to the behaviour atavistically dictated to them.

Among the Bantu and, indeed, among all primitive peoples, life and death are the great apostles of fidelity to a magical view of life and of recourse to traditional magical practices.

2. All human behaviour depends upon a system of principles.

If the modern over-civilized European is unable to be entirely emancipated from the attitudes of his ancestors, it is because his reactions are founded upon a complete philosophical system, influenced by Christianity ; upon a clear, complete, positive intellectual conception of the universe, of man, of life and death, and of the survival of a spiritual principle called the soul. This view of the visible and invisible world is too deeply ingrained in the spirit of Western culture, not to rise up again irresistibly when the great crises of life occur.

The German author and anthropologist Jahnneiz Jahn also dealt with the issue of a BLACK [African] PHILOSOPHY in his book - MUNTU : The New African Culture [New York, 1961] , pages 114 - 115 :

VI. RELIGION AND ETHICS

NTU is the universe of forces; it is not fitted to be the object of worship. And neither can the mythological representative of this universe, 'God' as Nya-Murunga, 'the great begetter', as *Olorun, Amma, Vidye, Immana, Bon Dieu* or whatever the representative of the world order happens to be called, be brought into a personal relationship with man. Complaints and wishes are not directed to the world order itself; a woman who pleads to have a child does not want any change in the fundamental laws of the cosmos. With one's personal cares and wishes one turns to the ancestors, above all to those who are strongest among them, founders of whole lines or special, famous ancestors, whose life, embroidered with legends, already has supernatural splendour. And these privileged ancestors, to whom a special cult is devoted, and who acquire increased force through the worship of many people—these ancestors become gods, 'orishas', as the Yoruba expression calls them. 'An orisha', writes Beier, 'is honoured not for his virtue but for his vitality. It is the intensity of life that attracts men to Shango. When they pray to him, they share in his life force, it helps them to achieve a higher life. At the same time the forces of the orisha are rejuvenated by the prayers, and so the community helps to build up and enlarge his powers; the Yoruba word for prayer is " She orisha", to "make" the God.'[51]

Yet, we have the following from an indigenous African anthropologist, President Jomo Kenyatta, in his book - FACING MT. KENYA [New York, 1969], pages 224 - 225:

THE CONCEPTION OF A DEITY[1]

The Gikuyu believes in one God, Ngai, the creator and giver of all things. *Ngai moombi wa indo ciothe na mohei kerende indo ciothe.* He has no father, mother, or companion of any kind. His work is done in solitude. *Ngai ndere ithe kana nyina, ndere gethia kana gethethwa.* He loves or hates people according to their behaviour. The creator lives in the sky. *Ngai eikaraga matuine,* but has temporary homes on earth, situated on mountains, where he may rest during his visits. The visits are made with a view to his carrying out a kind of "general inspection," *koroora thi,* and to bring blessings and punishments to the people. *Korehere ando kiguni kana gitei.*

The common name used in speaking of the Supreme Being is Ngai; this name is used by three neighbouring tribes, the Masai, the Gikuyu, and Wakamba. In prayers and sacrifices Ngai is addressed by the Gikuyu as Mwene-Nyaga (possessor of brightness). This name is associated with Kere-Nyaga (the Gikuyu name for Mount Kenya), which means: That which possesses brightness, or mountain of brightness.

The mountain of brightness is believed by the Gikuyu to be Ngai's official resting-place, and in their prayers they turn towards Kere-Nyaga and, with their hands raised towards it, they offer their sacrifices, taking the mountain to be the holy earthly dwelling-place of Ngai. *Kenyórorokero na kehuroko kia Mwene-Nyaga*—literally, "descending and resting- or dwelling-place of God."

The Being thus described cannot be seen by ordinary mortal eyes. He is a distant Being and takes but little interest in individuals in their daily walks of life. Yet at the crises of their lives he is invariably called upon. At the birth, initiation, marriage, and death of every Gikuyu, communication is established on his behalf with Ngai. The ceremonies for these four events leave no doubt as to the importance of the spiritual assistance which is essential to them.

The following from another indigenous African, Professor E. Bolagi Idowu, work of major note - AFRICAN TRADITIONAL RELIGION: A DEFINITION [New York, 1973] tells the story in the same manner as the above, which you could clearly observe is contrary to the RACIST and BIGOTED RELIGIOUS propaganda European and European-American so-called "CHRISTIAN MIS-SIONARIES" have been writing, teaching and preaching about over the last four hundred years:

The existence of Olódùmarè eternally[3] has, for all practical purposes, been taken for granted as a fact beyond question. It is upon this basic faith that the whole superstructure of Yoruba belief rests.

---

1. Note that "NGAI" is as much a "GOD" as is YWH/JEHOVAH, JESUS [the Christ], and/or AL'LAH of the HEBREW/JEWISH, CHRISTIAN, and/or MUSLIM/MOSLEM religion.

43

THE "NEGRO CHURCH": ASPECTS OF ITS ORIGIN:

On the other hand the African-American Professor Joseph R. Washington, Jr. wrote the following in his book - BLACK RELIGION: The Negro and Christianity in the United States [Boston, 1964], pages xi - xii:

> Black Religion is not a dispassionate, erudite treatment of the Negro and his American Christian tradition. It is not unique as a criticism of white institutional influences within religion in general and Negro responses to Christianity in particular. But Black Religion is, I believe, the first work which challenges simultaneously and equally white and Negro congregations and denominations to close the gap between creed and deed. What hopefully makes this book unique is its revelation of the weaknesses in Negro qua Negro religious life. The Negro and his religion are here taken seriously because to fail to do so only protects the Negro by hiding his failures, by treating him as immature. Respect comes when it is assumed people are mature enough to answer charges and responsible enough to meet a negative challenge with positive change.
>
> Hithertofore, American whites harbored overwhelmingly romantic notions about both the exotic and the unusually deep religious character of Christians who are Negroes. Negroes have known better but felt it to be high treason to lay bare the realities. The nonviolent movement and its development in the southern churches of the drive for civil rights has practically made Negro congregations "untouchables," organizations not to be criticized. A lieutenant in the SCLC could not get past the first chapter of Black Religion and was so incensed that on a radio interview he declared that I had given ammunition to the critics of the movement.
>
> Many whites have felt that Black Religion's criticisms of Negro religious life are precisely the criticisms they would make of their own churches. They have asked what is "new"? The answer is: nothing in practice; a great deal in purpose and meaning. Negro congregations have become less than their original intention demanded—by accident rather than design, by poverty rather than by an overabundance of well-being, by a paucity of rootedness and widespread uprootedness.
>
> If the overstatements in this book stimulate both people and institutions to change, this is sufficient reason not to rework the text. These pages are, I believe, filled with essentially correct destructive indictments. If Negro religious institutions are to continue to exist they need a purpose for existing meaningfully. It is now my hope to soon write as a complement to Black Religion a constructive statement suggesting a theology, a destiny, and a hope for Negroes in religious structures.   Joseph R. Washington, Jr.

The late Honorable Prophet and Pan-Africanist President-General Elect of the

Universal Negro Improvement Association and African Communities League, Inc.[UNIA]

44

noted the following in his book - PHILOSOPHY AND OPINIONS OF MARCUS GARVEY [edited and published by his second wife, Amy Jacques Garvey, London, 1924], pages 29 - 30:

Man's Kinship With His Creator

Christmas symbolizes something other than the amusement that it affords today. Christmas brings us to the realization of the fact that hundreds of years ago, when man was practically lost in his spiritual kinship with his Creator and the world probably was to be wiped away, the Son of God Himself came down from His throne on high for the purpose of saving you and saving me. We rejected Him in the past; our attitude now suggests no better consideration for Him if He should return, but with that patience, but with that love, but with that mercy, with that charity that caused Him to look down, not in revenge, but in the belief, in the hope, that some time man will change his ways—man will get to realize his true kinship with his Creator and be what his God expected him to be.

But before we reach this point we need a better understanding of self, as individuals, and may I not appeal to the strong and mighty races and nations of the world for a better and a closer consideration and understanding of the teachings of the man Christ, who went about this world in His effort to redeem fallen man? May I not say to the strong, may I not say to the powerful, that until you change your ways there will be no salvation, there will be no redemption, there will be no seeing God face to face? God is just, God is love, God is no respecter of persons; God does not uphold advantage and abuse to His own people; God created mankind to the same rights and privileges and the same opportunities, and before man can see his God, man will have to measure up in that love, in that brotherhood that He desired us to realize and know as taught to us by His Son Jesus.

Let us realize that we are our brother's keeper; let us realize that we are of one blood, created of one nation to worship God the common Father. It does not, therefore, suggest a proper understanding of our God or a proper knowledge of ourselves when in our strength we attempt to abuse and oppress the weak—as is done to Negroes today.

The Selfishness of Mankind

The statesmen of the world cry out for peace. They are meeting in many conferences with the hope that they will have peace; but I wonder if they understand the meaning of peace. There can be no peace until that peace reflects the spirit of the message of the angels of nineteen centuries ago. The real peace actuated by love, love as the Christ came to the world to give us; love for the high and mighty, love for the meek and lowly, love for all is the only peace that will reign, is the only peace that will draw man nearer to his God.

Albert Cleage, Jr., known today as Mwalimu Jaramogi Abebe Agyeman, preferred to put it in the following words in his book - BLACK CHRISTIAN NATIONALISM [New York, 1972], pages 4-5:

We Define Our Faith
The Black Nation

Generations of Black Christians have found inspiration in the tale of Israel's escape from bondage in Egypt without realizing that the Biblical Nation Israel was a Black Nation.* As Black Christian Nationalists in the twentieth century, we do not debate this historic fact, we merely

---
* Present-day white Jews were converted to Judaism in Europe and Asia following the fall of Jerusalem in A.D. 70.

Note: Not a single one of the Christian Clergy of the Black Church has written his own Black Bible.

assert it, because it serves to explain the African origins
of the basic religious myths and concepts of ancient Israel,
and also makes it possible to determine the historicity of
specific teachings attributed to the Black Messiah, Jesus,
in the Synoptic Gospels.

The New Testament reflects the primitive pagan distortions that the Apostle Paul foisted upon the early church
as a self-appointed apostle to the white gentile world.
Jesus was a revolutionary Black religious leader fighting
for the liberation of Israel. We can understand Jesus more
fully by looking at Moses and the Maccabees than by
looking at the Apostle Paul with his pagan concept of
blood redemption. The teachings of Jesus and of Israel
reflect the deep spirituality of Black people. The religious
ideas of Israel that shaped the ministry of Jesus can only
be understood in the light of the history and culture of
Africa.

Mwalimu Agyeman said what he had to say in quite eloquent terms indeed, and also

backed it with historical materials related to the African experience and birth of

Moses. However, on pages 57 and 58 he attacked the basic apathy of "NEGRO/WHITE

THEOLOGY" in the following terms:

We see every aspect of worship in a traditional Black
church contributing to Black enslavement. Many Black
Christians accept baptism as a mystery by which they are
changed in their relationship with God so that they can
escape from sin and the problems of life and fly away
home. They die to the old sinful life, putting aside petty
personal sins such as card playing, drinking, and fornicat-
ing. The entire experience has no meaning in terms of the
Black Liberation Struggle. In a world in which color de-
termines every aspect of their daily lives, conversion and
salvation are considered colorless. They are still going to
buy from white stores, vote for white candidates, and
straighten their hair in order to look like their oppressor.
They do not conceive of the Christian church involved
in a revolutionary struggle to liberate Black people from
the oppression of white people.

Dr. W. Hazaiah Williams, director of the Center for
Urban Black Studies in San Francisco, contends that the
Black church only appears to be otherworldly because it
defines worldly objectives in heavenly terminology easily
translated and understood by Black congregations. I wish
that this were true, but a Black congregation hears what a
Black preacher says, and only when the framework has
been clearly defined in terms of individual salvation are
they willing to ride the waves of sheer emotion with him,
in an ecstatic orgy of spirit in which coherent words only

46

serve to obscure rather than to clarity the message of a
personal salvation through Jesus. This kind of worship is
unquestionably a product of the Black experience, but
totally unrelated to the Black Liberation Struggle. Because
it diverts the Black man's attention from present ills and
serves as an emotional safety valve, it is not merely ir-
relevant, it is counterrevolutionary.

For Black Christian Nationalists, baptism symbolizes
dying to the old Uncle Tom ways and coming into a new
birth of understanding and commitment.

On page 174,under the sub-tittle "The Gospel Of Black Liberation", he placed
the issue "down front" with the following:

> A revolutionary Black church that seeks to explore new
> directions cannot hope to take everyone along on the
> journey. But certainly in a world in which people are dis-
> satisfied with the church—as most Black people are, be-
> cause they are finding less and less relevance in both its
> message and its program—there ought to be an increasing
> number of Black people willing to make the sacrifices
> necessary to structure a revolutionary church totally com-
> mitted to the Black Liberation Struggle.

All of the previously stated information can be examined and reexamined for
their content in a BLACK PHILOSOPHY that is universal for all of us. But it has to
be a "PHLDSOPHY" or "THEOLOGY" which does not specify a particular GOD-HEAD
with a singular NAME and/or SEX. For the "GOD" of a BLACK PHILOSOPHY and/or
THEOLOGY must be one [or more]UNIVERSAL DIVINITY in which all of us can relate
to without having to accept a special denomination's label.

Here is the major trouble spot of the UNIVERSAL BLACK PHILOSOPHY that
began with the TEACHINGS of the indigenous Africans of the Nile Valley and Great
Lakes regions of both North and Central Alkebu-lan. It is also the area in which we
must be able to see the commonality of all of Alkebulan's [Africa's] RELIGIONS from
North to South, East to West, and Central; thus from Africa's BOOK OF THE DEAD:

> ...To the great and supreme Power which made the
> heavens, the gods, the earth, the sea, the sky, men and
> women, birds, animals and creeping things, all that is and
> all that is yet to come into being, the Egyptians gave the
> name of *neter* ⌓⎤, or *nether* ⎯⎤, a word which
> survives in Coptic under the form *nuti* ⲛⲟⲩϯ. This word
> has been translated "god-like," "holy," "divine," "sacred,"
> "power," "strength," "force," "strong," "fortify," "mighty,"
> "protect," . .

---

1. This is true; but of little value without a "Black Bible" written by Black scribes.47

this being Black Theology   interpreted by a European. Thus, the salient points of <u>Pere Baudin's</u> [a Roman Catholic Missionary] observations about the African concept of "GOD" are shown in the following extract from his book - FETISHISM and WORSHIPERS - written in 1885 C.E./A.D. :

> In these religious systems, the idea of a God is fundamental; they believe in the existence of a supreme, primordial being, the lord of the universe, which is his work ... and notwithstanding the abundant testimony of the existence of God, it is practically only a vast pantheism – a participation of all elements of the divine nature which is as it were diffused throughout them all ... Although deeply imbued with polytheism, the blacks have not lost the idea of the true God: yet their idea of him is very confused and obscure ... God alone escapes both androgynism and conjugal association; nor have the blacks any statue or symbol to represent Him. He is considered the supreme primordial being, the author and the father of the gods and genii ... However, notwithstanding all these notions, the idea they have of God is most unworthy of His Divine Majesty. They represent that God, after having commenced the organization of the world, charged Qbatala[12] with the completion and government of it, retired and entered into an eternal rest, occupying Himself only with His own happiness: too great to interest Himself in the affairs of this world. He remains like a negro king, in a sleep of idleness ...[13]

Typical of the White Racist Nature of European-style "Christendom"; take note of the ending. From West Africa, particularly among the Yorubas of Nigeria, we have the following:

> What are we taught by our forbears, according to the oral traditions, about the world in which we live? Who made this world and all its fullness? And how are the affairs of the world managed?
> Someone who has made a careful study of all the material which our sources afford will have no hesitation in asserting that Olódùmarè is the origin and ground of all that is.[1] That is the fact which impresses itself upon us with the force of something incontrovertible. From all the evidence which we gather from the traditions, the Yoruba have never, strictly speaking, really thought further back than Olódùmarè, the Deity.

And from Central Africa, as interpreted by a European, the following:

> In *Africa and Christianity* Diedrich Westermann observes:
> In the centre of African myth stands a creative principle, which in most cases is identical with the high-god ... The high-god is, as a rule, not the object of a religious cult and is of small or almost no significance in practical religion. People acknowledge him, but neither fear nor love nor serve him, the feeling towards him being, at the highest, that of a dim awe or reverence. He is the God of the thoughtful, not of the crowd, of the people whose mature observation, personal experience, and primitive philosophy have led them to postulate a central and ultimate power who is the originator of everything existing and in whose hands the universe is safe: it is in the

The question is; to what extent are these indigenous AFRICAN/BLACK PHILOSOPHICAL THOUGHTS applicable to the AFRICAN/BLACK AMERICAN THEOLOGY of the late 20th Century C.E./A.D. ? To the extent that we can pick up our background history in the following from Professor <u>Cheikh Anta Diop</u>'s book - THE AFRICAN ORIGIN OF CIVILIZATION: MYTH OR REALITY [ed. by M. Cook, New York, 1973, pages 10 and 22:

Birth of the Negro Myth

> When Herodotus visited it, Egypt had already lost its independence a century earlier. Conquered by the Persians in 525, from then on it was continually dominated by the foreigner: after the Persians came the Macedonians under Alexander (333 B.C.), the Romans under Ju-

48

lius Caesar (50 B.C.), the Arabs in the seventh century, the Turks in the sixteenth century, the French with Napoleon, then the English at the end of the nineteenth century.

Ruined by all these successive invasions, Egypt, the cradle of civilization for 10,000 years while the rest of the world was steeped in barbarism, would no longer play a political role. Nevertheless, it would long continue to initiate the younger Mediterranean peoples (Greeks and Romans, among others) into the enlightenment of civilization. Throughout Antiquity it would remain the classic land where the Mediterranean peoples went on pilgrimages to drink at the fount of scientific, religious, moral, and social knowledge, the most ancient such knowledge that mankind had acquired.

Thus, all around the periphery of the Mediterranean, new civilizations have been built, one after the other, benefiting from the many advantages of the Mediterranean, a veritable crossroads in the world's best location. These new civilizations have evolved mainly toward materialistic and technical development. As the origin of that evolution, we must cite the materialistic genius of the Indo-Europeans: Greeks and Romans.

The pagan élan, which animated Greco-Roman civilization, died out about the fourth century. Two new factors, Christianity and the barbarian invasions, intruded on the old terrain of Western Europe and gave birth to a new civilization which today, in its turn, presents symptoms of exhaustion. Thanks to uninterrupted contacts between peoples, this latter civilization, which inherited all the technical progress of humanity, was already sufficiently equipped by the fifteenth century to plunge into the discovery and conquest of the world.

Some of us will argue that BLACK THEOLOGY must be denominational. Others will argue that it should be inter and intra-denominational. And still there will be so many who are too much afraid that their personal GOD-HEAD will loose specific publicity, and will insist that it be further identified as CHRISTIAN, JEWISH, MOSLEM, etc. The latter position is never threatened, no more so than the position of the "NEGRO" Judge in Raleigh, North Carolina who became infuriated at the mention of the name of the late Prophet Marcus Moziah Garvey; as he found it necessary to come to the aid of Washington, D.C. and announced to the hall full of young pledgees of a NEGRO" Greeks"FRATERNITY:[1]... "MY GRANDMOTHER WAS A WHITE WOMAN," etc., etc., etc.; and completed with his adopted WHITE RACIST CARETAKERS most common venom to those who disagree with the United States of America's "FOREIGN POLICY" towards the indigenous African People [BLACK LIKE THE JUDGE] and their governments in and out of the continent of Alkebu-lan ["Africa"] when he offered:...

"AN AIRLINE TICKET ONE WAY TO ANYONE WHO DOES NOT LIKE IT HERE IN THE UNITED STATES OF AMERICA, MY HOME, NOT YOURS."

---

1. The Greeks were civilized by Africans and Asians, yet African-American "fraternities" and "sororities" are copies of Greek immitation of African-Asian traditions.

What he has forgotten is that it took Rosa Parks, Malcolm "X", Martin Luther King, Jr., and the little unknowns who burnt buildings and broke storefronts all around the United States of America - from Harlem, New York City, N.Y., to Watts, Los Angeles, Calif. for all of us [himself included] to have our "NIGGER JOBS"; nothing but "TOKEN POSITIONS" of "POWERLESSNESS" when you balance all of US against OUR unemployed and unemployables, all of which includes being a "NEGRO JUDGE" in Raleigh, North Carolina.

In the "BLACK THEOLOGY" I am speaking about the Honourable Sis. [Mrs.] ROSA PARKS of Montgomery, Alabama will have to become a "SAINT". For what does one have to do in order to become a "SAINT"? Satisfy those who commissioned themselves the "AUTHORITY" of "SAINT MAKERS" by following certain well defined rules, dogmas and rituals agreed upon in a mythical structure; allegedly with "POWERS" granted it by a "GOD"! And if ROSA PARKS, the initial BRAIN THRUST or TRUSS who caused the Reverend Dr. Martin Luther King, Jr.[1] to reach NATIONAL and INTERNATIONAL prominence when she moved the so-called "CIVIL RIGHTS MOVEMENT" by refusing to sit in the so-called "NEGRO/NIGGER SECTION" on a bus in the City of Montgomery, Alabama is not a "SAINT" for this major exhibition of "BLACK [African] PRIDE" against the might of a "KU KLUX KLAN", this is due to the fact that WE have been programed everywhere in the United States of America to look at ourselves as "INFERIOR" - solely upon the basis of OUR "AFRICAN RACE" and/or "BLACK COLOR". But, why not a "SAINT" at least like the once most famous "SAINT CHRISTOPHER" of the Roman Catholic Church whom the Pope has since "de-SANCTIFIED" in the minds of those who formerly believed in him? Because it would mean that "SAINT JOHN, SAINT PETER, SAINT MARY, SAINT PAUL, SAINT AMBROSE" and all of the much more commonly known "CHRISTIAN SAINTS" will have to be reviewed to see what it is they have done with respect to their followers and national groupings that SAINT ROSA PARKS [like SAINTS FELICITA, PERPETUA and NYMPHAMO of Khart-Haddas or Carthage, Alkebu-lan or "Africa"] has not done for her African-American, African-Caribbean and African PEOPLE of the so-called "DIASPORA" in the Americas.

Revered ones like the late Rev. Richard Allen, Rev. Denmark Vessey, Rev./Prof. Henry Highland Garnett, Rev. Nat Turner, Rev. Absolom Jones, Rev. W. Palmer, Rev./Congressman Adam C. Powell, Rev. Malcolm "X", et al, all of whom preached a "BLACK THEOLOGY", along with members of their congregations like FREEDOM FIGHTERS Sis. Harriet Tubman, Sis. Sojourner Truth, Bro. Frederick Douglass and Bro. Booker T. Washington, et al must be at once and for all times designated "SAINTS" and "PROPHETS"

---

1. Pharaoh Akhenaten [ca. 1370 - 1352 B.C.E.] preached and practised "non-violent action" thousands of years before the birth of Mohandus Karamchand Ghandi, muchless the Reverend Martin Luther King, Jr. Akhenaten got rid of his army and allowed Egypt to be

50

at least, and "FATHERS" and "MOTHERS OF THE NEW BLACK CHURCH" and its "NEW BLACK THEOLOGY". Needless to say, the names I have mentioned are just a mere skimming at the top of the barrel of the hundreds of names to be added to the list. Or are we saying that:

ONLY THE POPES AND CARDINALS, HIGH PRIESTS AND BISHOPS, ALONG WITH CHIEF RABBIS, CAN MAKE "SAINTS" AND/OR "PROPHETS", etc. ?

If we are, please quote for my own edification just where in any of the "SACRED SCRIPTURES" of the Lord-God Jehovah, Jesus "the Christ", Al'lah, but not Lord-God Oledumare, Voodum, Ngai, et al, is such mentioned.

What all of this boils down to be is in the "nitty-gritty" POWER OF BLACK AUTHORITY OVER ALL THINGS BLACK - RELIGION INCLUDED AS MUCH AS OUR BLACK "GOD" and/or BLACK "HOLY FAMILY"[1] we must proclaim. This, of course, frightens the "HELL" out of those of us who can never do anything whatsoever without the guidance, control and/or approval of White "MASSA BOSS" and/or White "MISSI MAAM". So it is that our "NEGRO/COLORED" artists paint the same type of BLONDE, BLUE EYED, GOLDEN HAIRED, THIN LIPPED and POINTED NOSED European on the stained glass windows of any JET BLACK CHURCH with its equally 100 %/0 EBONY BLACK PARISHONERS to stare at in abject awe of their subconscious depth of RACIAL INFERIORITY. For there is no reason in all of this world that a WHITE CONGREGATION can be given that would make them accept from any WHITE ARTIST a THICK LIPPED, BROAD NOSED, WOOLLY HAIRED, EBONY SKINNED God of any religion known, or unknown, to date. Of course this will be tantamount to taking action to see as an ostrich does by placing its head in a hole and leaving its entire body out in the presence of danger. Thus we parrot the following:

"GOD HAS NO COLOR".

This psychosis is quickly eradicated. For it is obvious, at least it should be, that any "GOD" whatever must HAVE HAD, HAS NOW, or WILL HAVE in the very near future, a "COLOR" in order to HAVE BEEN SEEN by the Israelite PROPHET Moses, Christian GOD-HEAD Jesus "the Christ", the BAPTIST John, the DISCIPLE Peter and other DISCIPLES, et al who lived with Jesus.

The answer above naturally brings about the major task and hardest nut to crack in terms of a "NEW BLACK THEOLOGY" which would be accepted by the vast majority of the African People who are daily being mentally damaged and culturally brainwashed. For these acts of "SPIRITUAL GENOCIDE" are by no means different in a single way from those our ancestors were subjected to from ca. 1506 C.E. when the LILY WHITE ROMAN "CHURCH",

---

1. Not one solitary "Negro Religious Institution" has produced its own "VERSION" of any "HOLY/SACRED BIBLE" and/or "HOLY SCRIPTURES" to date in the U.S.A.

through the RACIST and RELIGIOUSLY BIGOTED mentality of Reverend [later Bishop] Bartolome de LasCasas and his Holy Father the Pope in Rome, Italy started the "IN-FAMOUS SLAVE TRADE" to the so-called "AMERICAS" and/or "NEW WORLD." Thus it is quite clear that what African People need today is...

A BRAND NEW BLACK BIBLE WRITTEN BY BLACK THEOLOGIANS, HISTORIANS, GEOGRAPHERS, ASTRONOMERS, ASTROLOGERS, PRO-PHETS, MATHEMATICIANS, METAPHICIANS, ETC.;JUST AS ALL OTHER RACIAL AND ETHNIC GROUPS HAVE DONE WHEN THEY WROTE THEIR OWN "MOST HOLY AND SACRED SCRIPTURES" FOR THEMSELVES [1] THEIR GODS AND GODDESSES,...

all of which we MUST adopt and classify as ..."GOD'S HOLY WORDS WRITTEN BY HIS MOST SACRED SCRIBES." Why? Because any and all of the "GODS" I have ever had the cause to read about had the same "IMAGE" as the people who wrote what I was reading about HIM or THEM. And said GOD-HEAD,or GOD-HEADS,is made to re-flect the hopes and aspirations of HIS scribes and other theologians. Yet if you have any doubt about this logic; why not read what has been said about "BLACK GODS" down through the ages even by "WHITE AUTHORITIES" such as the following:

Sir Godfrey Higgins' ANACALYPSIS [2 vols., 1840], Sir James Frazer's THE   GOLDEN BOUGH [13 vols., 1928], Albert Churchward's ORIGIN AND EVOLUTION OF RELIGION [London, 1921], Gerald Massey's BOOK OF THE BEGINNINGS [2 vols., 1930] and EGYPT THE LIGHT OF THE WORLD [New York, 1932], Gaston Maspero's THE DAWN OF CIVILIZA-TION [3 vols., London, 1888], Count C.F. Volney's RUINS OF EMPIRE [France, 1792] and Sir E.A.Wallis Budge's [edited and translated] EGYP-TIAN BOOK OF THE DEAD and PAPYRUS OF ANI [2 vols.].

There are so many thousands more I could have listed here, all attesting to each and everyone of "THE ORIGINAL GODS OF ANTIQUITY" being "BLACK" as the "Ace Of Spade" we use in playing our different types of card games. Quite a number of African and African-American AUTHORS/AUTHORITIES have also cited this historical "CARRY-OVER;" such as Professor George G. M. James' STOLEN LEGACY [New York, 1954] and Professor John G. Jackson's MAN, GOD AND CIVILIZATION [New York, 1973], and particularly in some of my own works: BLACK MAN OF THE NILE AND HIS FAMILY [1972], THE BLACK MAN'S RELIGION [1973, 3 vols], and AFRICA: MOTHER OF "WESTERN RELIGIONS" - JUDAISM, CHRISTIANITY AND ISLAM [1970].

The critical aspect in any kind of RELIGIOUS PHILOSOPHY [Black, White, etc.] is at all times the MYTHS and ALLEGORIES that comprise the EUPHORIA and MAGIC that created its "DIVINITY." All of this is accomplished through the SCRIBES and/or

THEOLOGIANS who recorded whatever the "DIVINITY" had, has and will have, to say in the BEGINNING OF TIME, DURING HIS PRE and BIBLICAL EXPERIENCE, and NOW IN THE POST BIBLICAL period. This is true for each and every RELIGION that existed and has since gone by the wayside, equally for all existing today - even YOURS and MINE, etc.!

As it stands today "NEGRO/COLORED THEOLOGY" taught in "NEGRO/COLOR-ED SEMINARIES" is as decadent as its LILY WHITE ANGLOSIZED, GRECO-ROMAN and ANGLO-AMERICANIZED "versions" from the beginning of the NICENE CONFER-ENCE OF BISHOPS [all 219 of them] in ca. 325 C.E.; at which time most of these men PLAGIARIZED and DISTORTED each and every page of SCRIPTURES of the Old Testa-ment and New Testament they retained, while SUPPRESSING each and every page they removed and destroyed, along with the others they have since labeled "LOST BOOKS OF THE BIBLE and THE FORGOTTEN BOOKS OF EDEN," and many other names.

Certainly we shall have to "GO DOWN [return] INTO EGYPT'S LAND;" but never to "TELL OLE PHARAOH" a single word about "LET MY PEOPLE" [Africans, African-American, African-Caribbeans or who else]"GO" unless we - AFRICAN PEOPLE - have made certain WE HEAR THE PHARAOH'S VERSION OF EXODUS other than that told by the other African superstar of the EXODUS DRAMA we call "MOSES."[1]For we must remember that the entire episode, supposedly, TOOK PLACE IN EGYPT, North Alkebu-lan between two groups, AFRICANS and AFRICAN-ASIANS,...those who wor-shipped AMEN-RA and those who worshipped YWH. There was not a single European or European-American, not even an INDO-EUROPEAN ARYAN, involved in this period ca. 1236 B.C.E. or XVIIth Dynasty demonstration of RELIGIOUS WARFARE between the Gods AMEN-RA and YWH in a moral story of "NATION BUILDING" - Israel; there being not a single "NATION" by this name during that period of time.

What make BLACK THEOLOGIANS feel that the WHITE THEOLOGIANS on pages 54-55 have some kind of a SACRED PEN or PENCIL from any place where they can-not equally purchase for money? The answer is in their DEEPLY ENGRAVED SENSE OF RELIGIOUS AND RACIAL INFERIORITY FROM THE INDOCTRINATION that ONLY WHITE PEOPLE CAN WRITE "GOD'S" HOLY SCRIPTURES," like we are witnessing in the following extracts from my own work - THE BLACK MAN'S RELIGION, EXTRACTS AND COMMENTS FROM THE HOLY BLACK BIBLE, page xvi Vol. I and xxiv Volume II, etc., all of which indicates that any group can make its own Biblical Authorities.

---

1. We need to remind ourselves that Moses/Moshe was an African, who God YWH turned his 'hands white as leprocy', the same as his sister Miriam, according to the Holy Bible.

Panel of Jewish Scholars Translating the Bible

Dr. Harry M. Orlinsky   Rabbi Solomon Grayzel   Photographs for The New York Times by JACK MANN
                                                      Rabbi Max Arzt

Rabbi Bernard J. Bamberger   Dr. H. L. Ginsberg

Translating Ezekiel 36:4

people; "therefore, ye mountains of Israel, hear the word of the Lord GOD: Thus saith the Lord GOD to the mountains and to the hills, to the streams and to the valleys, to the desolate wastes and to the cities that are forsaken, which are become a prey and derision to the residue of the nations that are found about; "therefore thus saith the Lord GOD: Surely

name was bandied about in the common talk of men. Therefore, listen to the words of the Lord GOD when he speaks to the mountains and hills, to the streams and valleys, to the desolate palaces and deserted cities, all plundered and despised by the rest of the nations round you. These are the words of the Lord GOD: In the fire of my jealousy I have spoken plainly

language and a butt for the jibes of every people ... truly, you mountains of Israel, hear the word of the Lord God: Thus said the Lord GOD to the mountains and the hills, to the water courses and the valleys, and to the desolate wastes and deserted cities which have become a prey and derision to the other nations round about: Surely, thus said the Lord GOD: I have surely spoken in My other and against all of Edom which,

The text at top is from the 1917 version by the Jewish Publication Society; the one at center from the New English Bible. In the revised draft agreed upon by the scholars, bottom, the single word "derision" was changed to "a laughingstock." The new translation is by Rabbi Harry Freedman.

Note: They made themselves their own "AUTHORITIES/HOLY SCRIBES", etc. in God's Holy Name. Maybe the pictures on p. 56 will remind them of their AFRICAN/BLACK origin biblically.

THE NEW YORK TIMES, TUESDAY, MAY 29, 1973

A Scholar Infers Jesus Practiced Magic

By ISRAEL SHENKER

In two books scheduled for publication this month, Prof. Morton Smith of Columbia University presents evidence that may alter understanding of the New Testament, of Christianity and of Jesus.

The books deal with a fragment of a purported secret Gospel of Mark, which Professor Smith discovered; a primitive text from which the Gospels of Mark and John may have been drawn; early Christian secret rites and their ties to pagan practices and Professor Smith's conclusion that Jesus practiced magic.

His evidence goes back to his discovery at Mar Saba, an ancient Greek Orthodox monastery near Jerusalem, of a manuscript purportedly the text of a letter from Clement of Alexandria.

Clement was one of the great fathers of the Church, and his writings date back to the end of the second century. This letter, in tiny Greek script on two pages that had been used as the last page and in the binding of a 17th-century book, was to a Theodore (not identified); it referred to what Clement said was a secret Gospel of Mark.

After consulting experts in paleography, Professor Smith announced his discovery in 1960. Since then he has been reaching some startling conclusions about the letter.

Theses Outlined

Harvard University Press is publishing the extended scholarly version of these finds and conclusions, entitled "Clement of Alexandria and a Secret Gospel of Mark." Harper & Row is publishing a layman's account entitled "The Secret Gospel." In an interview at his apartment here, Professor Smith, who has been teaching ancient history at Columbia since 1957, outlined the principal theses.

From the Mar Saba document, Professor Smith concluded that the early church in Alexandria was "a split-level group"; there were initiates privy to secret doctrine and a larger group of faithful who knew only public teaching.

"Everybody knows there were a lot of apocryphal

The New York Times/Meyer Liebowitz
Prof. Morton Smith of the Columbia University faculty

gospels besides the four canonical Gospels—Matthew, Mark, Luke and John," Professor Smith said. "But the notion that an orthodox congregation, such as the church of Clement, had an authoritative secret Gospel is new."

Primitive Source

The secret Gospel recounts a story Professor Smith sees as almost identical with the account that John expanded into the story of the raising of Lazarus from the dead. "It helps us complete a long line of parallels between Mark and John, filling the gap that existed," Professor Smith suggested. "The parallelism now continues from the sixth chapter of both Mark and John until the account of the Crucifixion."

Stylistically, the secret Gospel is close to the Bible's Gospel according to Mark.

and Professor Smith suggests there was a primitive gospel from which the books of Mark and John were both drawn.

"This would take us back well before the year 70," he suggested. "It would give us a notion of the Gospel circulating at or before the time of Paul, who is our earliest source for Christianity, and could thus be much closer to the time of Jesus than the canonical Gospels. This is not an outlandish possibility. Most scholars agree that the Gospels of Matthew and Luke are both taken from Mark."

Professor Smith credits Prof. Cyril C. Richardson, dean of graduate studies at Union Theological Seminary, with the breakthrough leading to the remaining conclusions. What Professor Rich-

ardson suggested was that Mark 10:13 to 10:45 closely reflects the content of an early baptismal service. (These passages deal with Jesus's blessing children, a rich, young ruler, rewards, Jesus's foretelling death and resurrection and responding to requests of James and John.)

"Professor Richardson's suggestion enables us to understand the nature of the initiation rite that the secret Gospel reports," Professor Smith said. "We now see that 'the mystery of the kingdom of God' is the content of baptism. The canonical Gospel's story [Mark 14:51-52] of a young man apprehended at night alone with Jesus at the time of Jesus's arrest (a story which scholars have puzzled over for 1,800 years), is now understandable as an account of a baptismal rite conducted by Jesus in which the believer united with Jesus and was possessed by his spirit.

"Once we have this report that Jesus administered a nocturnal, secret initiation, we naturally ask, 'Why nocturnal?' 'Why secret? Particularly if this was only a baptism?' What was going on?"

Schisms Noted

Professor Smith suggested that the answers could be determined from a consideration of the splits in early Christianity. Some Christians, he said, insisted on strict obedience to Jewish law, others argued for selective obedience, a third group declared itself emancipated from Jewish law and dedicated to guidance by the spirit and a fourth group was blatantly libertine.

Jesus himself violated Jewish law: he did not observe the Sabbath, he consorted with publicans and sinners, he did not fast, or wash his hands before eating. But at times he urged observance of the law.

Some scholars said that Jesus's words should be taken figuratively, others argued that the libertine texts were exaggerated or misunderstood and still others maintained that Jesus taught that moral law was binding.

The continuation of this article on the following page only indicates what I have been contending all along. "MAGIC" was as much a part of the RELIGIOUS BELIEFS of all RELIGIONS - including Judaism, Christianity and Islam - down through the ancient ages as it is today in 1978 C. E. And all of the incense burning and other types of MAGICAL INCANTATIONS, including the so-called "EVERLASTING LIGHT" burnt in synagogues and churches, also mosques, come directly from the worship of the Great God RA who was later called "AMEN-RA, AMEN-RE," etc. We see the RAISING OF THE DEAD for RESURRECTION and the HEREAFTER before its Judaeo-Christian-

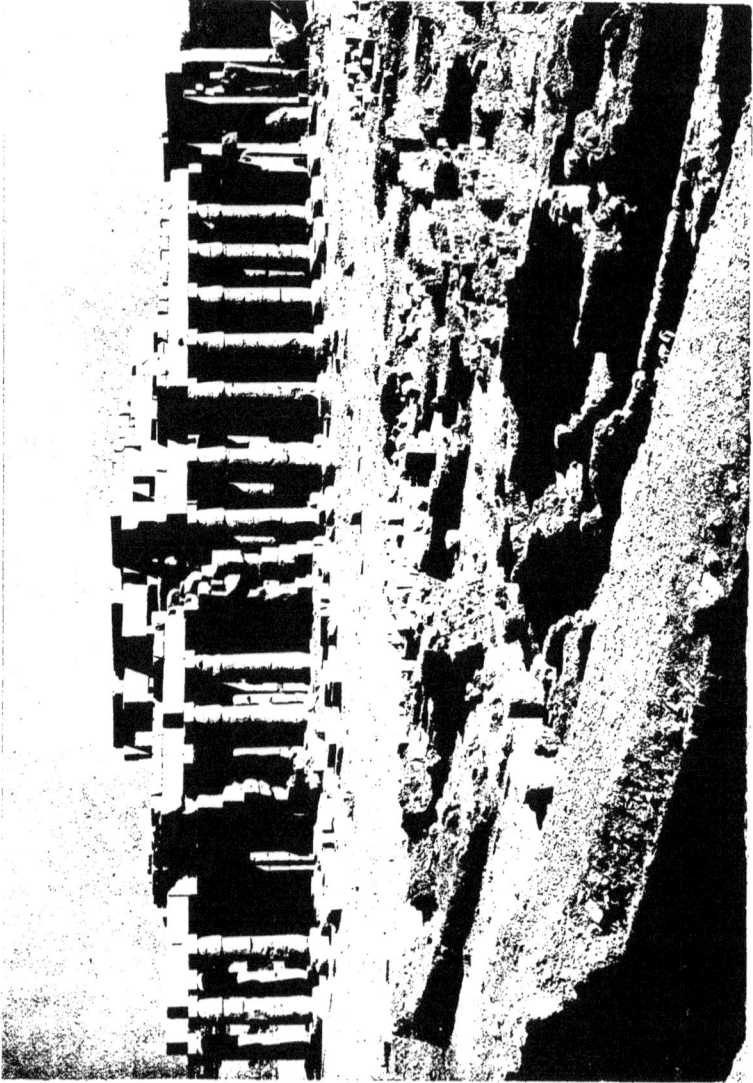

FUNERARY/TOMB OF PHARAOH RAMESES II WHO [allegedly] TRIED TO KILL MOSES IN ca. 1236 B.C.

TEMPLE, WITH VIEW OF THREE MAIN NAVES AND TWO SOUTHWESTERN LATERAL AISLES OF THE HALL OF PILLARS

FUNERARY TEMPLE/TOMB OF PHARAOH RAMESES II, ca. 1298 - 1232 B.C.E. AT THEBES

A view from the north showing STORE ROOOMS IN RUIN in the foreground

Islamic PLAGIARIZATION, DISTORTION and final ADOPTATION in the Five Books Of
Moses, New Testament and Holy Kor'an from the teachings the indigenous "BLACK
AFRICANS" of the Nile Valley and Great Lakes High-Cultures created in the Grand
Lodge of Luxor's Mysteries System. Just imagine, even this "WHITE AUTHORITY"
is not safe in telling the truth about religion without the cloak of acceptable insincerity –
otherwise known as "ACADEMIC TENURE" or "PERMANENT FIXTURE," etc.:

ritual law not.
Professor Smith argued that Jesus distinguished between levels of his following. For those already in the kingdom of heaven (thanks to secret baptism), the law was not binding. But Jesus urged others to respect the law.

How did Jesus persuade his intimates of his special position and of their membership in the heavenly elect? Professor Smith replied: "I believe the answer is that Jesus had a way with practiced some sort of hypnotic or suggestive discipline embodied in rituals derived from ancient magic.

"If you take as your task the problem of finding what social type Jesus is, in the gallery of figures provided by the Greco-Roman period, the best answer is the mira-

cle-working magician.

Magical Practices

Professor Smith compiled a long list of practices associated with magicians of antiquity and ascribed by the New Testament to Jesus—"the power to make anyone he wanted follow him, exorcism (even at a distance), remote control of spirits, giving disciples power over demons, miraculous cures of hysterical conditions including fever, paralysis, hemorrhage, deafness, blindness, loss of speech, raising the dead, stilling storms, walking on water, miraculously providing food, miraculous escapes, making himself invisible, foreknowledge, mind-reading, claiming to be a god or son of god or in image of god."

"All these claims and stories and rites are those of a magician, not of a rabbi or

a Messiah," Professor Smith notes in "The Secret Gospel." "Who ever heard of the Messiah's being an exorcist, let alone being eaten?"

Professor Smith noted that many of the powers claimed are paralleled by practices described in the so-called magical papyri—documents discovered in Egypt that report pagan practices. The magical papyrus most closely associated with a eucharistic-like practice deals with erotic magic. And the magical papyri as well as Jewish handbooks purport to explain the hypnotic technique allowing men to enjoy and transmit the illusion of ascent into heaven. "The stories of Jesus's resurrection seem distorted versions of such an illusory ascent," Professor Smith suggested.

A Time of Danger

"The spirit was at first the

spirit of Jesus, then gradually became independent of him and was eventually located in the Trinity," he went on, noting: "When the spirit went public the Apostles lost much of their control of the company and came into danger of displacement."

"If the Christians were an innocent sect practicing pure benevolence, why did the Romans make such strenuous efforts to stamp them out?" Professor Smith asked rhetorically, and replied: "It was because the Christians engaged in magical practices, and magic was a criminal act."

Professor Smith expects lively controversy about his findings, less from documents than from people.
"I'm reconciled to the attacks," he said. "Thank God I have tenure."

The following MAGICAL RELIGIOUS RITE is only one of the many hundreds Jesus Christ
had to learn and practice when he received his education and initiation from African teachers
in North Africa's MYSTERIES SYSTEM while he lived in Egypt and Nubia.

SHADOW AND SOUL LEAVING THE TOMB [1]

... from the rubric we learn that a figure of it was to
be made in gold and fastened to the neck of the
deceased, and that another, drawn upon new papyrus,
was to be placed under his head. If this be done
"then shall abundant warmth be in him throughout,
"even like that which was in him when he was upon
"earth. And he shall become like a god in the under-

"world, and he shall never be turned back at any of
"the gates thereof." The words of the chapter have
great protective power (i.e., are a charm of the greatest
importance) we are told, " for it was made by the cow
"for her son Ilâ when he was setting, and when his
"habitation was surrounded by a company of beings of fire."

1. See PAPYRUS OF ANI [as transl. by Sir E.A. Wallis Budge]. The scribe Ani passing through
the door of his tomb; his shadow and "heart-Soul" remains outside.

Note: We must realize that all of the "miracles" attributed to Moses, Jesus, Mohamet
et al of Judaism, Christianity and Islam were done by others before them.

But are we admitting that all of the so-called "AUTHORITIES" on the <u>Old Testament</u> and "AUTHORITIES" on the <u>New Testament</u> we have been led to accept are teaching in our "NEGRO/COLORED SEMENARIES" only for "MAKE BELIEVE"? Are we further saying that the LILY WHITE RACIST "HOLY FAMILY" and LILY WHITE RACIST HEAVEN FULL OF PURE WHITE ANGELS, and the occasional JET BLACK DEVIL that relates to the story of HOW BLACKS GOT THEIR COLOR from Ham's story with respect to the <u>Great Deluge</u> [flood], are in fact the "TRUE" and "MOST SACRED TEACHINGS OF GOD" [anyone of them]? If not, why can we not stop this LILY WHITE RACIST MYTH and IMAGE from further corrupting the minds of our children to turn out future SELF-HATERS amongst us? "FEAR" of our WHITE AUTHORITY in WHITE THEOLOGY; and all because we <u>had not</u> [<u>have not</u>, and obviously will not have] DONE our own homework and research to find OUR OWN TRUTH. Tell me what it is about the following WHITE MARY/and JESUS which my BLACK SELF can identify.

Mary Nursing The "Christ-Child"
Origin ca. 1976 years ago

Origin ca. 6075 years ago

ISIS and the Infant HORUS,
BLACK MADONNA & CHILD
[r.W. Petrie Coll.]

Why I cannot equally identify with the Black ISIS and HORUS/OSIRIS they copied long before you call this aspect of "BLACK THEOLOGY" your usual "CURSE WORD" you have reserved for the "ANTI-CHRIST, ANTI-JEHOVAH, ANTI-AL'LAH," and even the plain old "ANTI-GOD" you feel you must destroy for an obviously HELPLESS GOD who needs your intervention to protect "HIS IMAGE?" The answer follows. It is, because We need a "BLACK PHILOSOPHY;" not a verneered ASPHALT COATED WHITE THEOLOGY of the left-over GRECO-ROMAN-GERMANO-ENGLISH-WELCH type that was, and still is, linked and associated with the INFAMOUS SLAVE TRADE, colonization of the so-called "NON-WHITE WORLD," investor world wide cartels and international conglamorates and land annexations through neo-colonial WARFARE.Such an all BLACK THEOLOGY will not accomplish any more than our current "NEGRO/COLORED THEOLOGY" has ever since the word "AFRICAN" was removed from our own institutions and substituted with the word "NEGRO" and/or "COLORED." The mental state which brought us to DENY OUR AFRICAN HERITAGE, even OUR INDENTIFICATION AS AN AFRICAN PEOPLE, equally took away OUR DIGNITY AS A RACE. Thus our failure to had developed a BLACK PHILOSOPHY that would have surely supported a BLACK THEOLOGY that is so badly needed in our PHYSICAL and CULTURAL REVOLUTION in our SELF-AWARENESS that "BLACK IS" in fact "BEAUTIFUL". The same BLACKNESS and BEAUTY to which I allude are not only that AESTHETICAL SKIN-DEEP TONE we wear on our outer-self; but instead the "BLACK BEAUTY" we created along the Great Lakes Regions of Central Alkebu-lan ["Africa"] and spread throughout the entire ancient world as we move down the Blue and White Nile River Valley developing what was to become our ZENITH in Punt, Itiopi, Meröe, Ta-Nehisi, Ta-Merry and turned westward to Lebus, Numidia, Khart-Haddas and Mauritania.[1]·Of course I cannot neglect the fact that we had equally moved southerly and built our CONE TOWER ALTAR to our Gods, and into Monomotapa [including Swaziland] to MINE our minerals, following which we even traveled northwest to create our Benin,Fa,Ife,Ijaw and other kingdoms of the Edoh Empire in conjunction with that of Nzaide all the way past Ashante and then into Mauritania once again, etc.; all of which you witnessed in just a few artifacts from our illustrious past on the following pages - 61 - 62, and others shown before.

As I close my appeal to my fellow African [BLACK] Educators, whose duty it is to lead our people to a RIGHTEOUSNESS FREE FROM ANY FORM OF INFERIORITY COMPLEX, I ask of you:

HOW IS THIS POSSIBLE WITHOUT A BLACK THEOLOGY OF OUR OWN?

1. This was the African Empire that produced the original Moors who built Europe's first SCHOOL OF HIGHTER EDUCATION   "Universidad de Salamanca in Spain."

<u>GOD'S "HOLY/SACRED PLACES":</u>

THE "BLACK MINDS, HANDS AND WORKERS THAT CREATED AND BUILT THESE
PYRAMIDS AND CANDACES ALSO CREATED THE "BLACK THEOLOGY AND THE-
OSOPHY" THAT WERE RESPONSIBLE FOR THAT OF JUDAISM, CHRISTIANITY
AND ISLAM, ETC.

CEMETERY PYRAMIDS and CANDACES
of Meröe and Ta-Nehisi

[Photo: Museum of Fine Arts, Boston, Mass.]

Foreground: SOUTHERN MECROPOLIS - IIIrd Century B.C.E.
Background: NORTHERN MECROPOLIS - IVth Century B.C.E. to C.E.

COLOSSAL Step Pyramid of Sakhara,
by Pharaoh Djoser, IIIrd Dynasty;
architect and builder Imhotep.

MEDIUM Pyramid of Ghiza, by Pharaoh
Snefru, IVth Dynasty.

One will notice that the PYRAMIDS got larger, and to the point of becoming COLOSSAL,
as the indigenous Africans High-Cultures [civilizations] of the Nile Valleys [blue and
white] traveled farther NORTH from their SOUTHERN origin. Obviously, the different
types of construction materials the indigenous Africans employed in the above pyramids
were not in any sense "MUD AND STRAW BRICKS" after the IIIrd Dynasty, c. 2780
B.C.E.; they were GIGANTIC STONES up until the IVth Dynasty, c. 2680 B.C.E. Even
as late as the IIIrd to Ist century B.C.E. the indigenous Nile Valley Africans were
still building their homes in the NETHER WORLD [pyramids or tombs] in the manner
typically of their Great Lakes origin around Central East Africa.

Note that the IIIrd Dynasty STEP PYRAMID of Pharaoh Djoser [Zozer] and his architect - IMHOTEP- influenced the dominant design of pyramids all through the VIth Dynasty; this we can readily notice in the MEDIUM PYRAMID of Pharaoh Snefru above.

COMPARE PHARAOH SNEFRU'S PYRAMID WITH THAT OF PHARAOH [King]
ASKIA AND OTHERS OF THE ASKIA DYNASTY ON PAGE 48 OF THIS WORK

61

BUILT BY BLACK HANDS, DIRECTED BY BLACK MINDS WHICH
PRODUCED THE WORSHIP FOR A "BLACK GOD" IN "AFRICA"
The [cone shaped pyramid] Temple Of God

SOME ANTIQUITIES OF ZIMBABWE

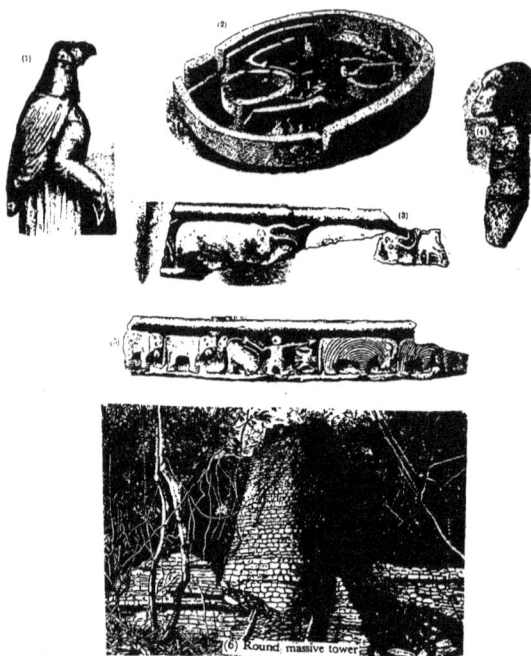

(1) Vulture's head; (2) Model of ruins; (3) Oxen; (4) Head of man;
(5) Hunt (the hunter is shown as suffering from steatopygia)

From J.C. deGraft-Johnson, AFRICAN GLORY, London,
1954, page 52, etc.

Note the majesty of the architectural beauty and astetic richness of the Africans of Monomotapa, Alkebu-lan. The engineering achievment demonstrated
in this structure has never been surpassed in any of ancient Ta-Merry, Ta-
Nehisi, Itiopi, Numidia, Khart-Haddas or Puanit, etc.

THE SACRED WRITINGS ABOVE THE CONE TOWER ARE RELATED TO THE
BLACK THEOLOGY AND BLACK GOD OF THE AFRICANS OF ALKEBU-LAN
THAT PREDATED THE JUDAEO-CHRISTIAN-ISLAMIC ADAM

The worshipers of <u>Amen-Ra</u> have the following saying in their BLACK THEOLOGY, etc.:

"THE FUNDAMENTAL TEACHINGS OF SALVATION MOST IMPORTANT OB-
JECTIVE IS THE...DEIFICATION OF MAN...;"

and if liberated from its bodily abode the "SOUL OF MAN" could enable him/her to be in real-

ity "GOD-LIKE". As such...

"MAN WOULD BE AMONG THE GODS IN HIS LIFETIME ON EARTH AND AT-
TAIN VISION IN HOLY COMMUNION WITH THE IMMORTALS THAT BE"....

The worshipers of YWH [Jehovah] have the following teaching about their BLACK THE-

OLOGY:

> ₃ [Ethiopia]   Ah, land of buzzing insects, beyond the rivers of Ethiopia, ₂
> sending ambassadors by sea, in papyrus boats on the waters! Go, swift
> messengers, to a nation tall and bronzed, to a people dreaded near and
> far, a nation strong and conquering, whose land is washed by rivers.
> All who inhabit the world, who dwell on earth, when the signal is raised
> on the mountain, look! When the trumpet blows, listen!
> ₄   For thus says the Lord to me: "I will quietly look on from where I
> dwell, like the glowing heat of sunshine. like a cloud of dew at harvest
> time. ₅ [ISAIAH, Chapter xviii, Verses 1 - 7]

The worshipers of JESUS ['the Christ'] have the following teaching about their BLACK

THEOLOGY according to Augustine ["Santos" or "Saint"], CITY OF GOD, Book XIX, Chapter 14:

> But as this divine Master inculcates two
> precepts - the love of God and the love of
> our neighbor - and as in these precepts a
> man finds three things he has to love - God,
> himself and his neighbors - and that he who
> loves God loves himself thereby, it follows
> that he must endeavour to get his neighbor
> to love God, since he is ordered to love
> his neighbor as himself.

The worshipers of AL'LAH have the following poetical teaching about their BLACK

THEOLOGY - promised in the KORAN [see J.A. Rogers' WORLD'S GREAT MEN OF COLOR,

Volume I, etc.]:

> "...seventy-two of these lustily beautiful
> creatures" (Black-eyed daughters) " are given
> to every" (Male) "believer, who himself will
> possess eternal youth and vigor."
>
> They have beautiful, well-rounded bodies,
> fresh with the eternal youth and virginity
> that is constantly renewed.

The worshipers of VOODUM have the following teaching in their BLACK THEOLOGY
according to Reverend Godfrey Parrinder explaining the Dogon's religion in his book -
AFRICAN MYTHOLOGY - etc.:

> In the beginning of the **one God, Amma,** creat-
> ed the sun and moon like pots, **his first** inven-
> tion. The sun is white hot and **surrounded by** eight
> rings of red copper, and the **moon is the same**
> shape with rings of white copper. The stars came
> from pellets of clay that Amma flung into space.

The worshipers of OLEDUMARE have the following teaching in their BLACK THE-

OLOGY according to E.B. Idowu's OLODUMARE: GOD IN YORUBA BELIEF, etc.:

63

Then there are the divinities,[4] especially tne principal ones. All the indications which have come down to us are that they were all brought into existence by Olódùmarè that they might be His ministers in carrying out, each in his own office, the functions connected with the creation and theocratic government of the earth. But as to when they began to be, we have little information. They are first introduced to us in connection with the creation of the earth and the arrangement of its equipment.

The worshipers of NGAI complete this reflective background in BLACK THEOLOGY with the Most Sacred God Inspired Holy Scriptures in Jomo Kenyatta's FACING MT. KENYA, etc.:

> According to tne tribal legend, We are told
> that in the beginning of things, when mankind
> started to populate the earth, the man Gikuyu,
> the founder of the tribe, was called by the Mo-
> gai (the Divider of the Universe), and was giv-
> en as his share the land with ravines, the riv-
> ers, the forests, the game and all the gifts
> that the Lord of Nature (Mogai) bestowed on man.
> kind. At the same time, Mogai made a big moun-

And everyone of these, as all of the other GODS I have quoted before along with their worship- ers, can be packaged into the following maxim our AFRICAN [Black] ANCESTORS who wor- shiped RA stated before any of the other GODS mentioned, equally as those not mentioned, had their origin in Alkebu-lan, Asia, Europe, the "Americas", Australia, and elsewhere:

"MAN [African, Black," Negro, Colored, Bantu," etc.] KNOW YOURSELF".

JESUS "the Christ" ENTRANCE INTO JERUSALEM ACCORDING TO A FIFTH CENTURY C.E./A.D. ETHIOPIAN MANUSCRIPT [Biblio-theque Nationale, Paris, France. A Black original with All Blacks]

Is it from Genesis 3: 1 – 24 the SERPENT allegory or the Nile Valley PHALLIC CREATION Worship it all began? The SERPENT in was in RELIGION 360 years before JUDAISM, CHRISTIANITY, and/or ISLAM

Scene from the PAPYRUS OF HER–UBEN

Note that the Africans showed the "MANHOOD/PENIS" of the DECEASED relative to the value of LIFE before and after DEATH. You will note that the PENIS has been omitted in most of the same scenes shown in most of the "Western Textbooks" in order to meet the hypocracy of so-called "PONOGRAPHY." Also, the SNAKE is symbolic of the PENIS – and holds the same meaning in the original ADAM AND EVE allegory in GENESIS.

65

Osiris and the Egyptian Resurrection

In the Ptolemaïc Period some interesting additions appear in the scenes in which Osiris plays the chief part. Thus, in a relief at Denderah,[1] the god, arrayed in a garment which reaches to his ankles, stands holding his symbols of sovereignty. Before him stands "Horus, son of Isis and Osiris," holding a knife in his left hand. Between the god and his father is the terrible "slave stick" Y, which is stuck in the ground, and to it is tied by the arms an ass-headed man in a kneeling position. Three knives stick in his stomach. This

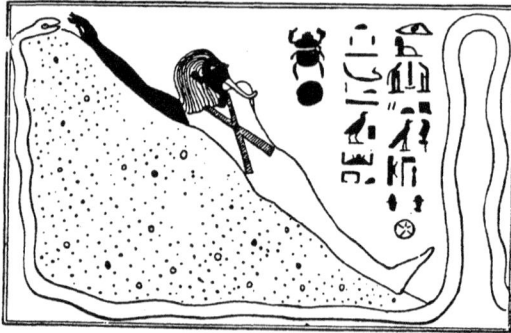

Osiris-Res, or "Osiris the Riser."

figure, of course, represents Set, who has been vanquished and wounded by Horus and his sons. In another relief Khenti-Åmenti is given the head of the hawk of Seker,[2] and thus Osiris represents the ancient gods of the dead of Busiris, Memphis, and Abydos. In another relief are given the seven forms of Osiris as follows :—

    1. Osiris in Ḥet-Ṭeṭet, i.e., the Temple of Busiris.[3]
       He holds in his hands a sceptre bearing the

[1] Mariette, Dendérah, tom. IV, Plate 56.
[2] Ibid., Plate 38.
[3] ⬚⬚⬚ ⬚⬚⬚⬚⬚ , Mariette, Dendérah, tom. IV, Plate 89.

Extracted from page 46 of E.A.W. Budge's
OSIRIS: THE RELIGION OF RESURRECTION
[University Press, Hyde Park, New York,
1961]. Note the omission of the "PENIS" in
this picture to suit the perverted view about
the reproductive organs by "Westerners".

Note: See Genesis, Chapter I - III for distortions of the above, particularly as it is shown on p. 65.

THE "CROSS": A CHRISTIAN DISTORTION
OF BLACK THEOLOGY'S "ANKH":

Symbolically the "ANKH," which has been transformed into the early "CHRIS-
TIAN CROSS" sometime following the death of the Christians GOD–HEAD Jesus, must
return to its truest character in the BLACK THEOLOGY in which it was created and
developed within the MYSTERIES SYSTEM; just as it will have to be in a new BLACK
THEOLOGY, irrespective of the other distorted forms below and on the following three
pages - 68, 69 and 70:

pilaster-cross

Ethiopian

Coptic

The "BLACK MESSIAH" Ascension, according to a Fifteenth Century, C.E.
Ethiopian manuscript in the Bibliotheque
Nationale, Paris France.[Note the typical
elongated art-style common throughout
Africa from the reign of Pharaoh Amenhotep IVth/Akhenaten, ca. 1370-1352 BC].

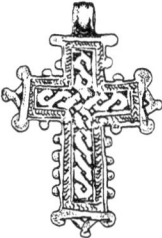

pectoral crosses   *filigree crosses*

For a history of "The Origin Of The Cross"

see Y. ben-Jochannan's Black Man Of The Nile And His Family, pages 361 378,   etc.

Nile Valley "ANKH" or "CROSS"

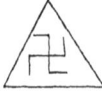

"Druids" Swastika from Egypt

SYMBOLS OF THE DIVISION OF HEAVEN, REPRESENTING HORUS AND SET AND HORUS, SET AND SHU WITH SWASTIKA OF THE FOUR QUARTERS.

Lanteglos Churchyard, Cornwall Ank Cross

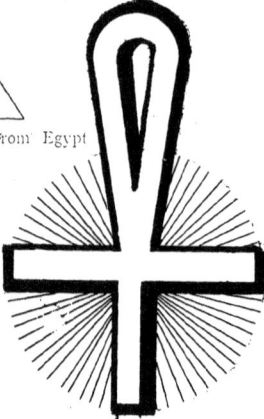

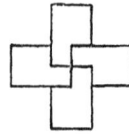

Solar mythos Cross, the 4 quarters is depicted as Atun-Ra

1. The so-called "OLD TESTAMENT CROSS", otherwise known as the "SAINT ANTHONY CROSS," was used by the earliest European Christians of Rome in the Catacombs under the name of "CRUX COMMISSA" or "TAU CROSS." Most of the 18th through 20th century C.E. European and European-American "Christian" theologians refer to this CROSS as the "TYPE CROSS" T. The "TAU CROSS" received its name from the erroneous translation by European scholars who believed that the Africans' ANKH was equivalent in value to their fellow Europeans of Greece's letter of the alphabet - TAU. This error was no different to what they had done with respect to the musical sign of the same Africans of Egypt and Nubia's NEFER 𝄞 or 𝄞 , which they held represented a "...LATIN CROSS..." or "...UPSIDE-DOWN ANKH..." with the meaning of "SORROW."[See Schliemann, MYCENAE AND TIRYNS, p. 66; Baring-Gould, MYTHS OF THE MIDDLE AGES, p. 358; Payne Knight, SYMBOL LANGUAGE, p. 238; Wilkerson, ANCIENT EGYPT, iii, p. 362; Munter, RELIGION der BABYLONIER, Kopenhagen, 1827; Louisa Twining, SYMBOLS OF EARLY AND MEDIAEVAL CHRISTIAN ARTS].

Some historians of "SEMITIC ORIGIN" even refer to their own books of religious mythology and quote from EZEKIEL, ix, 14, where it is stated that their God, YAWEH or JEHOVAH, etc., sent Ezekiel to Jerusalem "...TO SET A MARK UPON THE FOREHEADS..." of certain males [Jews] as a sign of their "...RIGHTEOUSNESS AND EXCEPTION FROM JOHOVAH'S WRATH...," etc. This gave rise to their translation of the word "MARK" in Hebrew to be the equivalent of the Greek "TAU" or hithwîthâ tau; thus, their association of it to the so-called "TAU CROSS."

COPTIC AMULETS   On the stele of ABRAHAM (B.M., No. 1257) we have it in this form with the letters ⟨ and Ω. On the stele of PLÊINÔS (B.M., No. 679) we have the ordinary Greek cross , the 𝗫 and two ânkh crosses

On the stele of SABINOS (B.M. 1352) we have 𝗫 and ⟨ and Ω. On another stele are cut figures of doves holding ☥ (B.M., 1327). NAVILLE found a mummy with the suwastika drawn on the left shoulder (see Deir el-Bahari, ii, p. 5), but there is no proof that the mummy was that of a Christian.

THIS "ANKH" CREATED THE BLACK THEOLOGY FOR THE EVER-SEEING EYE OF HORUS AND HOUSE OF THE GOD RA ON THE U.S.A's ONE DOLLAR BILL TO D. TE

LIKE THE "ANKH" THE  GRAMMADON [Swastika] WAS
USED IN BLACK THE- OLOGY FOR A SIGN OF HOLY

Egyptian Swastika

THE CROSS—ITS ORIGIN, DEVELOPMENT AND INTERPRETATION

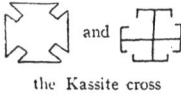 and

the Kassite cross

Saint George of Lydda.

A group of Crosses in gold, steel and Limoges enamel.

☧ = Χριστός, or ⚹ = the initials of Ἰησοῦς Χριστός, or ⳨ = chi-ro

the so-called monogram of Christ

Tracings of the magical forms of the Cross found in an Ethiopian Book of
the Dead called "Lefáfä Şedək" (Brit. Mus. MS. Add. 16204).

ETHIOPIAN AMULETS

PEACE LIKE THE "DOG STAR" ON THE FOLLOWING PAGE

69

As we noticed the distortions of the "ANKH" increased with the time-periods closer to our own contemporary era; thus we should have equally noticed the commonality in the distortions of the following "DOG STAR" and/or "TUAT"..., etc...

"THE TUAT AND THE TWELVE HOURS OF THE NIGHT"

This is the "Ever-seeing Eye of Horus and House/Pyramid of God Ra which you witnessed on the △ United States of America's One Dollar Note [see green side of of this currency/bank note, etc.]

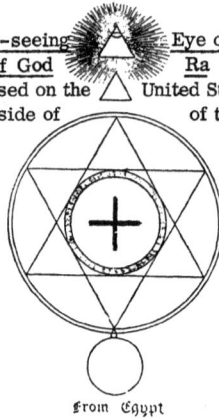

from Egypt

into what was to be later called a "MOGEN DAVID" or "STAR OF DAVID"···

related to the Hebrew God-Head "YWH" or "JEHOVAH" [Hieroglyph ⬚⬚⬚⬚ , in Hebrew ⬚⬚⬚ or ⬚⬚ , in Greek ⬚⬚⬚⬚ , and Latin DEO] and PHARAOH [King] DAVID over the Kingdom of Judea [Israel]. But there was no "STAR" in David's honor; thus our equal BRAINWASHING by Jewish sources like those I have already shown on page 54.

This work's priority is the highlight of a decadent "COLORED/NEGRO-WHITE THEOLOGY" that outdated its usefulness because of its NONFEASANCE and MALFEASANCE. Thus it is that I see no reason why "CHRISTIANITY" cannot be as viably meaningful in this 20th Century C.E. NUCLEAR AGE without the perpetuation of a "VIRGIN

BIRTH" due to an "IMMACULATE CONCEPTION" today in 1978 C.E. For we must remember that this allegory dates back only to the past 1978 years ago, but is no older than 1628 years in any reality; it having started at the NICENE CONFERENCE OF BISHOPS in ca. 325 C.E. Obviously we do not need this TABOO anymore so than we needed "DEMONS" and "MONSTERS" in our "HOLY SCRIPTURES" for DIVINE INTERVENTION. We do not, for we have always conducted our FERTILITY RITUALS in terms of the reality of a God who loves and respects LIFE and DEATH in the same proportion; since man LIVES and must DIE, which we can see in the MAGICAL-RELIGIOUS "LIFE-DEATH" DIVINE INTERVENTION being conducted by our African-Australian BLACK[1.] brothers below:

Here mankind looked for an approach at paying homage to the FERTILITY ORGANS

See H.W. Smith's MAN AND HIS GODS; Sir J. Frazier's THE GOLDEN BOUGH [13 vols.]; A. Churchward's THE ORIGIN AND EVOLUTION OF RELIGION; G. Maspero's THE DAWN OF CIVILIZATION; M. Muller's THE SACRED BOOKS OF THE EAST; R. Bell's INTRODUCTION TO THE QUR'AN; A.C. Bouquet's COMPARATIVE RELIGION; E. James' COMPARATIVE RELIGION; B. Malinowski's MAGIC, SCIENCE AND RELIGION AND OTHER ESSAYS; and A. Waley's THE AMALECTS OF CONFUCIUS.

This brings us to the main character in the drama that initiated this work - Jesus ["the Christ"] and his LIFE-DEATH episode. But it was the LIFE ON EARTH of Jesus which millions of people adore that made his NAME become a household WORD. His education in the MYSTERIES SYSTEM along the Nile Valley and in the Lodges of the Grand Lodge of Luxor such as RAISING of people from the depths of degradation, FEEDING of the multitude and PROTECTION of the defamed and humiliated in the face of power were only a very choice few of the very many ACTS OF COMPASSIONATE HUMAN QUALITIES the moral stories about his LIFE ON EARTH emphasize.

1. Throughout "Western/White Academia" it is still being taught that "...the aboriginal Australians have nothing in common racially with Negro Americans...",

It was not Jesus' "DEATH ON CALVARY'S CROSS" depicted below in the center of the Ethiopian CRUCIFIX CROSS which made him important; but instead his LIVING EXAMPLE. For there were two others being equally LYNCHED or CRUCIFIED by the Jewish and Roman mob in Romanized fashion - NAILED TO A CROSS and allowed to bake into DEATH'S AGONY by the firery "SUN RAYS" of the God "ATEN" which Pharaoh Akhenaten and others thousands of years before recognized as the "MANIFESTATION OF THE ONE AND ONLY SACRED BEING." This we can see as plain as day is to night when anyone we have loving knowledge of passes away into the stage of life we call "DEATH." But we, seemingly, MUST persist in this manner; solely because we want so badly to BELIEVE that our own physical presence will be preserved for ANOTHER WORLD somewhere beyond this current understanding. Yet here is the juncture of suspense when we should be asking ourselves:

WHO AMONGST US DEFINITELY KNOWS ABOUT "HEAVEN" OR "HELL"? But then, if we do, we must face the reality of a possible NON-EXISTENCE following the cessation of the pumping motion of the HEART and the bellowing of the LUNGS in the LIFE-DEATH struggle in which we are engaged.

VARIATIONS OF THE AFRICANS' ANKH-CROSS[1].

Certainly it is truly "FEAR OF THE UNKNOWN" that the CRUCIFIX above represents. "FEAR" makes most , if in fact not all, of us BELIEVE in a "HERE-

1. Why not a single Black Minister is teaching his parishioners that the use of the use of the "Cross" in religion preceded Jesus "the Christ" by thousands of years .

AFTER" or "NETHER WORLD, " etc. some of us even break down into "HELL" for
the UNGODLY [including everyone except myself] who has always refused to accept

[The "Last Judgment" bass-relief on the Cathedral of Orvieto, Italy with
its Devil and his Demons that date back thousands of years before Jesus]

any "HEAVEN" for the GODLY, which included myself in the middle of everything going
on with the other SAINTS, ANGELS,etc. And FEAR even created the two scenes here.

[Heaven or "Abraham's Bosom" according to The Gospel Of St. Luke,
xvi: 22, showing angels carrying the redeemed souls up to Abraham,
who accepts them for God...? In the Cathedral Of Reims 13th Century
C.E. painting. Note that all of the SOULS are white as Abraham et al]

But we do not BELIEVE that these totally different extreme positions within our FAITH
SYSTEM continue because of those who are constantly playing with our FEAR that we
WILL NOT ENTER HEAVEN and/or WILL ENTER HELL, all of which is perpetuated
by those whose LIFE-STYLE and PROFESSION it is to benefit economically therefrom.

1. Why can't Black Ministers commission Black Artists to paint Black religious scenes?
    Inferiority.

ETHIOPIAN CHRISTIAN VERSION OF THE "ANKH" and "DOG STAR" or "TUAT"

FROM A BLACK COUNTRY AND A "BLACK THEOLOGY" WE DO NOT KNOW.
WHY?

The Nuptials of Cana, from a fifteenth century manuscript. (Photo Bibliothèque Nationale)

Note that the same elongated style was used by Pharaoh Akhenaten in ca. 1370 - 1352 B.C., also that this allegedly proved his "monstrocity": thick lips, broad nose, etc.

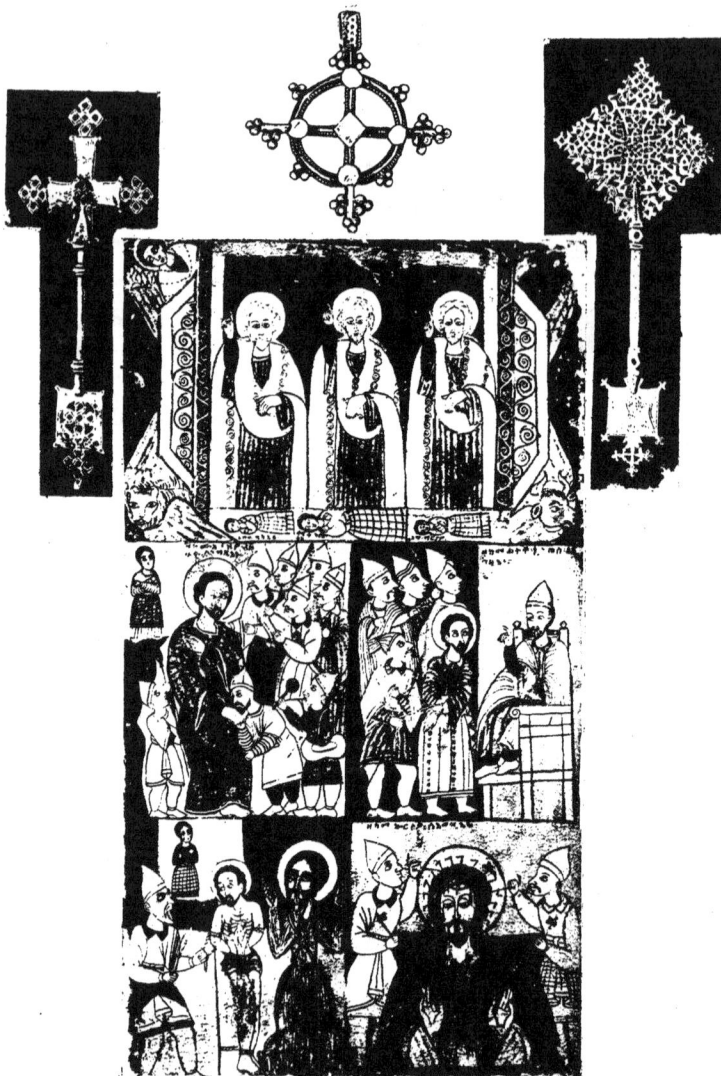

AN ETHIOPIAN ARTIST STORY OF "JESUS the CHRIST" AND HIS FAITH IN THE ELONGATED
ART FORM STYLE MADE COMMON BY PHARAOH AKHENATEN, ET AL

TRI-CROSSES LECTERN OF THE TRINITARIAN SAINTS OF ETHIOPIA
Left to Right: St. Tekla Haymanot, St. Ewostatewos, St. Gabra Manfas
Qiddus. This brass lectern had a third cross [missing from the lunette
over the center figure]. The lectern is dated somewhere between ca. 15th
and 18th Century C.E. These are some of the most important Saints.

"GO FORTH CELEBRATING IN JOY THE MESSAGE OF YOUR GOD"[Pharaoh Akhenaten]

DANCE OF THE CROSS. ONE OF THE MOST ANCIENT OF THE
CHRISTIAN RELIGION'S FESTIVAL DANCES IN HONOR OF THE
BIRTH, LIFE, DEATH AND RESURRECTION
OF JESUS "THE CHRIST"
Ethiopia, Alkebu-lan

Roman Emperor Honorious - of African-European parentage [From a painting by the noted French painter Jean Paul Laurens]. Of similar birth as Emperor Septimus Severus and his son Emperor Caracalla.

"Near these approaching with his radiant car
The sun their skins with dusky tint doth dye
And sooty hue; and with unvarying forms of fire
Crisps their tufted locks." 1

. From the ancient Greek writer Theodectes describing the Ethiopians COLOR and HAIR,,

HE IS PART OF THE "BLACK THEOLOGY" THAT WAS OF EARLY CHRISTIANITY

79

GOD'S "RACIAL/ETHNIC Identity.

Everyone of us -   AFRICAN [Black] PEOPLE - should notice that the WHITE
MYTHOLOGY'S HELL is ugly and totally distorted in the sense of BIBLICAL DEMON-
OLOGY, which in color is full of BLACK; whereas not a single person in the HEAVEN-
LY MYTHOLOGY is equally BLACK, not even an occasional ANGEL in transit from or
to "HELL. This is, of course, unless we are dealing with an ETHIOPIAN HEAVEN like
the following from an early Christian manuscript in the Bibliotheque Nationale, Paris:[1.]

And providing we can see very plainly the total BLACKNESS of the African tradition in
presenting "GOD" like the people whose artists reduced their DIVINITY to paint, and
material of a solid nature as those I cited on the following page compared against
the other HEAVEN I showed on page 67 dealing with the ancension.

I am more than convinced that GOD is a "RACIST" and "RELIGIOUS BIGOT"
whose only feelings and teachings are those placed into "HIM" or "IT" by male authors
who are labeled "PROPHETS, SCRIBES, DISCIPLES, " etc.; all of whom those of us
who followed hundreds of years later went beyond and added to their titles the following:

"DIVINELY INSPIRED, SACRED, HOLY, GODLY, "
etc. with a host of other superlatives, not one of which we can find enough verbiage to
clearly and adequately define just what we mean by said nomenclatures.

HE or IT - God - is of a SPECIFIC RACE and COLOR. This is to any normal

1. Why can't this picture become typical in Black Churches throughout the U.S.A. ?
   Because the Black Clergy lack the necessary "BLACK THEOLOGY".

ALL OF THESE PEOPLE ARE "BLACK" AS THEIR OWN GOD

The THREE SHEPHERDS ["Wise Men"] VISITING THE JESUS CHILD

The THREE SHEPHERDS ["Wise Men"] TRAVELING TO VISIT THE
JESUS CHILD
[From an Ethiopian manuscript of earliest Christianity presently in
the Bibliotheque Nationale, Paris, France. How did they get there?]

person who is proud of his or her heritage, as we see this commonly demonstrated in the heavenly scene called "EZEKIEL'S VISION OF THE VALLEY OF THE DRY BONES" where the deceased has been raised to life in European/ Semitic WHITE:

[Fresco by Herbert J. Gute, 3rd Century C.E. in a Dura Europos Synagogue Mural under the tittle "THE VISION OF EZEKIEL, also in Yale University Art Galery, New Haven Connecticut. Racist; is this not so?]

In the following from a Buddhist metamorphosis by Chinese artists we see the resurrected evolving Chinese YELLOW from his wicked BLACK past:

[From the Temple Of The Sleeping Buddha, Suchow, China. Notice the SNAKE changing its skin in the water of the deep spoken of in the Judaeo-Christian-Islamic allegorical story in our GENESIS:]

We see our ONE AND ONLY TRUE GOD not as a "SPIRIT," but as a PHYSICAL MANIFISTATION of that which he or she desires to be in the THEN and NOW, even before our experience in any place call "HEAVEN" and/or "HELL." This is no different from the experience any FATHER has when he sees his newly born CHILD for the first

82

time. Of course this is not exclusive of any MOTHER when she sees her SON in the IMAGE OF HIS FATHER and her DAUGHTER in the IMAGE OF HERSELF. All of these emotions are transfered to our "GOD" in our normal "CARRY-OVER" from our socio-political culturization to its ultimate expression of the "DEIFICATION" process we carry forward each and every day. This we do in our "ANCESTRAL WORSHIP" which others prefer to do for that which they label "SPIRIT WORLD, SAINTS, ANGELS", and even "DIVINE ONES." Thus we find living amongst us "SAINTS" in many denominations or sects of the "CHRISTIAN FAITH" or "RELIGION" who even adopted one of the most noted of the so-called PAGAN CUSTOMS" of the ancient world that preceded the Judaeo-Christian -Islamic mistique;...

"TALKING IN TONGUES"....

This of course must relate to the TOWER OF BABEL[1] shown below in the background of the HANGING GARDENS OF BABYLON according to a restoration sketch by an artist:

But it is only in respect to those who have been PSYCHED-UP enough after an ectasy with "HIM" or "IT" can experience. This has to be; for the TOWER OF BABEL was not even as tall as the Ethiopian monolith of more than ten stories high , which I have shown on the following page. Yet, in this experience should we not hear the voice of "HIM" or "IT" - God - and be able to transcribe or orally deliver said "GOOD NEWS"

---

1. Nowhere is there a single stone or brick of Tower of Bable available as proof of its existence.

to those of us less fortunate enough to BELIEVE but not
blessed with this "SPECIAL CALLING"? NO! Because the
cold hard-fast fact is that neither those "SPEAKING IN
TONGUE" and those who are not during this "SPIRITUAL
ORGY" could consciously repeat and/or tell of a single
THOUGHT or FEELING during this episode physically or
mentally. Yet we continue BELIEVING in its allegedly
"MAGICAL" and/or "DIVINE" spirituality. If this is
equally required of any "JEW, CHRISTIAN, MOSLEM," et
al before he or she considers him or herself "SAVED, GOD-
LY, RELIGIOUS, CHOSEN," etc. this kind of RELIGIOUS
EXPERIENCE should hardly be expected to catch the imagination of young people who stare down the focusing eye-
piece of a microscope in any high school and/or college la-
boratory looking at "GOD" the sperms and ovum.

I refuse to accept either the "VIRGIN " state of
Mary's MOTHER when she gave birth to her; of Mary's "IM-
MACULATE CONCEPTION" when she became pregnant with
Jesus for Joseph or the "angel of the Lord;" and the "VIRGIN
BIRTH OF JESUS" out of the womb, down through the fallopi-
an tube, and through the orifice protected by the HYMEN that
blocks the way to the passage for physical sexual intercourse which we are to believe remained intact in the case
of Mary's pregnancy. Moreso, that it was possible for Mary
to again become "CONCEIVED" with Jesus' BROTHERS and
SISTERS and still her PHYSICAL VIRGINITY remained in-
tact.Yes, NONE of this is needed for a MAN like JESUS.

I do not need the MYTHOLOGY and/or ALLEGORY of
the story about Jesus' life-style no more so than that of any of the other SIXTEEN
CRUCIFIED SAVIORS, including the first one of them all - OSIRIS/HORUS, in order
to be able to follow the REVOLUTIONARY ACTION he took against a corrupted state
and cajoling members of the national religion. But could we not see the need for such
a frame of reference in the so-called "WATERGATE INCIDENT" that involved one of

1. The African genius that created the Pyramid in Egypt equally created this in Ethiopia.

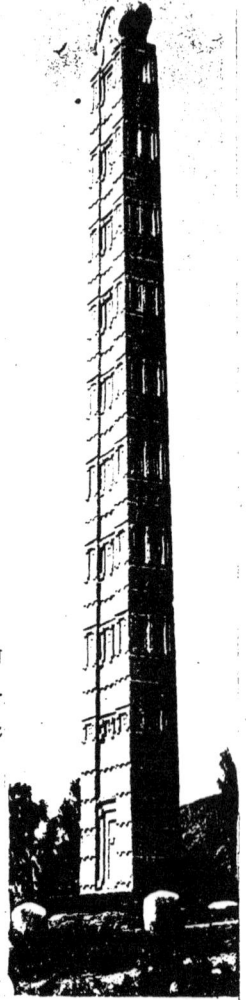

THE OBELISK OF ON

Note: On was renamed "Heliopolis" by the Macedonian-Greek conquerors of Egypt in ca. 332 B.C.E.

The above is typical of the previous page, and common to the African/Black People of the ancient Nile Valley High-Culture/Civilization that originated in Central Alkebu-lan and branched out all over the entire continent before the coming of the very first "White/Caucasian/Semitic Man and/or Woman" to any part of Alkebu-lan.

The caraftsmanship which produced the above, equally those before and following in this volume, came from indigenous African/Alkebu-lanian who reached their "zenith" in Egypt.

the United States of America's most noted self-proclaimed "EVANGELISTS"[God Inspired Christian theologians and revivalists],along with a retired Jewish Rabbi who still swears for his willo-the-whist machivillian former PRESIDENT of the United States of America's "INNOCENCE", while the evidence overcomes them with its quality and quantity? Yes we did! But we can no more reject this than the fact that...

GEORGE WASHINGTON WAS A RACIST SLAVEMASTER OF AFRICANS,
THUS NO FATHER OF THE "NEGROES FREEDOM" OR LAND; ...

nor that the same condition holds true for our most famous LIBERTARIAN - Thomas Jefferson - who equally had a notorious SLAVE FARM full of Africans up to and until his last breath of life. You see, we too have been conditioned by our BRAINWASHING culturally as we are RELIGIOUSLY by the same source and media. The controlers of our ECONOMIC and CULTURAL LIFE-STYLE equally control the RADIO and TELEVISION we listen to and look at, also the NEWSPAPER and other READING MATTER in our initial experiences with an EDUCATION [moreso miseducation] from the cradle to the grave.All of this is true whether RELIGIOUSLY or SECULARLY. But not a solitary word of it can we freely accept unless we are equally willing to challenge "the powers that be" like Jesus did against "uncle tom puppets" of the Kingdom of Israel and their colonizers from Rome under the rule of the Caesars [Kings, Emperors, etc.].

The "JESUS" I am interested in following according to life-style is only the HUMAN BEING who "FLOGGED THE MONEY CHANGERS" involved in the business of conducting their banking in the synagogue. Not a "JESUS" who appears as a placid HOMOSEXUAL in a spotless WHITE ROBE, immaculately combed hippy-style GOLDEN HAIR, perfectly MANICURED NAILS and OILED HANDS without a solitary blister from serving his fellowman; and even at age "THIRTY-THREE" without the benefit of a normal human male desire for a SEXUAL RELATIONSHIP with any of the thousands of women around him in a POLYGAMOUS CIVILIZATION where each and every man of his era had a generous number of."wives, concubines, harlots, whores," and whatever else. The entire crux of the SEXLESS LIFE OF JESUS, whether from Mary's CONCEPTION through divine activity of the ANGEL OF THE LORD, his VIRGIN BIRTH and final ADULT EXPERIENCES all the way until his DEATH ON CALVARY's CROSS, I cannot see the need for said IMAGE. This is due to the fact that I found in MENTAL and PHYSICAL SEXUAL INTERCOURSE, CONCEPTION or PREGNANCY with or without marriage, childbearing and childbirth, the highest manifestation of "GOD" in his, her, it, they or whatever else GLORIOUS HEAVEN. For in what other manner can MAN

JUST IMAGINE !

IT HAPPENED IN "DARKEST AFRICA", SOUTH OF THE SAHARA.

"MAN" BEFORE THE JUDAEO-CHRISTIAN-ISLAMIC "ADAM" IN THE GARDEN
OF EDEN" SOMEWHERE IN ASIA

RECONSTRUCTION OF FOSSIL-MAN

(Top) Reconstruction of
Zinjanthropus boisie
(African fossil-man)

(Top) A sculptured at-
tempt at reconstructing
Neanderthal man (Euro-
pean fossil-man).

Full figure attempt
by
Maurice Wilson

(Bottom) Skull of Zin-
janthropus boisie un-
earthed in Bed I of Ol
Olduvai Gorge, Tangan-
yika, by Dr's. L.S. &
M. Leakey.

(Bottom) An attempt in
paint. Both by Maurice
Wilson.

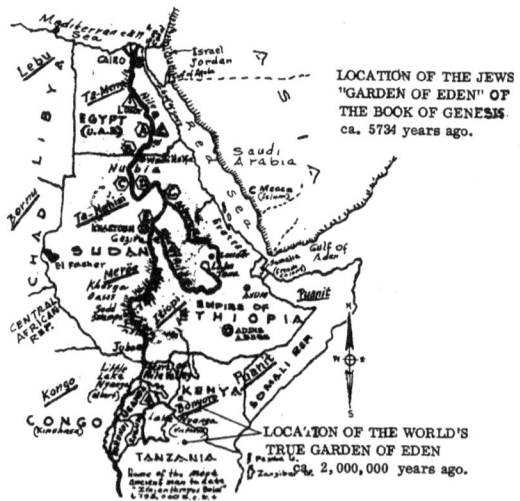

LOCATION OF THE JEWS
"GARDEN OF EDEN" OF
THE BOOK OF GENESIS
ca. 5734 years ago.

LOCATION OF THE WORLD'S
TRUE GARDEN OF EDEN
2,000,000 years ago.

THE NILE VALLEYS AND GREAT LAKES REGION
1969 C.F.

.THIS FACT DEMANDS A "BLACK THEOLOGY" FOR THE "FIVE BOOKS OF MOSES,
PARTICULARLY "THE FIRST" [Genesis]

be created and/or born...

"IN THE IMAGE OF GOD"?....

Here I place my BELIEF as a worshiper of the GODS Amen-Ra, Ywh, Jesus ["the Christ"] or Al'lah," and of course not excluding the thousands more all over the planet earth. Here I can empathize with Joseph as a FATHER, Mary as a MOTHER, and Jesus as their most precious SON or GODLY CREATION who became their third part or "TRINITY." Yes, this "TRINITARIAN DRAMA" is repeated every second of each and every day all over this entire planet earth wherever God's "CHOSEN PEOPLE" [each and everyone of us] are. "GOD" -- male "sperms" and female "ovum", etc!

Certainly I cannot BELIEVE that a woman's biological usage of her VAGINA in a normal healthy PHYSICAL SEXUAL INTERCOURSE that resulted in the rupture of her HYMEN or VIRGINITY before marriage defiles her entire body. I do not think I could have BELIEVED this if I were living back there 1974 years ago with MARY and her man JOSEPH, or even 5748 years ago with ADAM AND EVE in the "Garden Of Eden" somewhere in Asia, and even before that 1,750,000 years ago with ZINJANTHROPUS BOISE and his WOMAN in Central Alkebu-lan's HOME OF THE ORIGINAL HUMAN BEING I have shown on page 82 with the original "GARDEN OF EDEN" called the "OLDUVAI GORGE"... or with our so-called "PYGMIES" which the Europeans and

FIG. 64.
MONGUNGU. MATUHA. BOHANI.

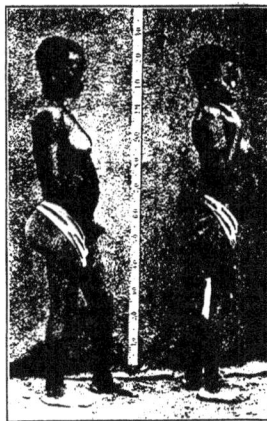

FIG. 65.
KUARHE. AMOORIAPE.

[Reproduced from Dr. G. Elliot Smith's article in The Lancet]

European-Americans of WHITE ACADEMIA have now claimed to be "LITTLE WHITES" or "BLANQUITOS" [in BLACK sheep's skin as I have shown on the previous page].Yes, just as I began on page xxii under the heading - "PRELUDE" - so shall I end with the clearest of determination that African [BLACK] People, like all other racial peoples, MUST have...

"WEIGHING OF ANI'S HEART AGAINST THE FEATHER OF TRUTH", . . .

[Ani before Osiris]   [Gods in the Chamber of the Gods]

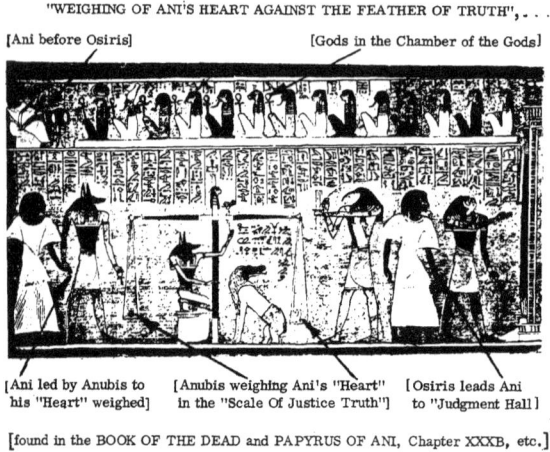

[Ani led by Anubis to   [Anubis weighing Ani's "Heart"   [Osiris leads Ani
his "Heart" weighed]   in the "Scale Of Justice Truth"]   to "Judgment Hall]

[found in the BOOK OF THE DEAD and PAPYRUS OF ANI, Chapter XXXB, etc.]¹·

1. The hieroglyphic inscription tells of the deceased scribe named Ani getting his "Heart" weighed preparatory to entering the "NETHER WORLD" [Heaven]. See English traslation by Sir Ernest A. Wallis Budge's BOOK OF THE DEAD and PAPYRUS OF ANI, Chapter XXXB; also y. bзn-Jocherman's BLACK MAN OF THE NILE AND HIS FAMILY, p. 122.

and OUR OWN BLACK THEOLOGY BASED UPON OUR OWN BLACK PHILSOPHY... in order to serve OUR OWN BLACK DIVINITY as shown above, and according to the SACRED AND MOST HOLY SRCIPTURES that remind us of the following:

"AND THE LORD YOUR GOD MADE MAN IN HIS OWN IMAGE."

But most of all, let us AFRICAN/BLACK PEOPLE not forget that:

All faith is FALSE, all faith is TRUE
TRUTH is the shattered mirrors strewn
In myriad bits; while each BELIEVES
his LITTLE BIT the whole to own.¹

1. From: "The Kasidah of Haji Abu el-Yezdi;" as translated by Sir Richard F. Burton

RACISM IN "SACRED/HOLY PLACES"
EVEN IN "GOD'S HOLY HOUSE/CHURCH":

In dealing with the ART OBJECTS [paintings, carvings, etc.], SIGNS, SYM-
BOLS and TALISMANS of the Judaeo-Christian-Islamic religions we must relate
back to the ancient indigenous African [BLACK] People whom certain "MODERN
[European and European-American] ACADEMICIANS" prefer to call "PYGMIES"
[Blanquitos or "Little Whites"], irrespective of their many appearances on pages
37 and 38. If we follow this pattern of approach, we will soon find that the answers
lead along a trail that would have an origin on the banks of the Blue and White NILE
with all of its High-Cultures and BLACK PEOPLE from the south. Yet it is only Ta-
Merry that the vast majority of European and European-American "SCHOLARS" and
their African, African-American and African-Caribbean "UNDERSTUDIES" have con-
sistently insisted was the "ORIGINAL SOURCE." Why? Because the Greeks and Romans, both of whom were brought into "CIVILIZED LIVING" by the indigenous Afri
cans of Egypt,   based their entire existence intellectually on their "STOLEN
LEGACY" from the MYSTERIES SYSTEM, all of which the current WHITE RACE has
adopted as being "CONTRIBUTIONS OF WESTERN CIVILIZATION."[i] Yet the ancient
Greeks and Romans themselves claimed very little as their own ORIGIN; but not their
descendants who followed centuries later all over Europe and European-America.
Thus it is that European-Americans for the past two centuries have attributed every
development of the Africans all along the Nile [BLUE and WHITE] River and Great
Lakes region as being "EGYPTIAN. These conquerors have purposely and completely overlooked all that they saw of the same CONTRIBUTIONS of the Africans of Ethi-
opia to Egypt, including their EARLIEST CHRISTIAN DOCTRINES - THEOSOPHY, THE-
OLOGY, TABOOS, MYTHS, ALLEGORIES, etc. This is no different than they did
to the indigenous so-called "BLACK AFRICANS" of Egypt in making them "ASIAN [white]
SEMITES" and "ISRAELITES'   in terms of the FOUNDING OF JUDAISM and the
creation and development of what is today called "THE FIVE BOOKS OF MOSES" [Old
Testament, Holy Torah, Comesh, Pentateuch, etc. They suppressed acts that the EGYP-
TIANS themselves attributed their own EXISTENCE and HIGH-CULTURE [civilization]
to their BLACK ANCESTORS of predynastic Egypt [Ta-Merry, Kemit, Sais, etc.] at...
    "THE BEGINNING OF THE NILE WHERE THE GOD HAPI DWELLS AT
    THE FOOTHILLS OF THE MOUNTAIN OF THE MOON" [Kilamanjaro].
The same reason exists today as WHITE theologians and academicians of every

---

I. High Culture is a preferred term to the White Racist nomenclature... civilizations...

type constantly attribute ETHIOPIA'S ORIGINAL FORMS OF CHRISTIAN SYMBOLS to Europeans who came into Egypt and seized the COPTIC branch of the ancient Christian order; many of which you have already seen in this volume on pages 67 - 72 , etc.

For example, the "ETHIOPIAN CRUCIFIXES" and other "CROSSES" related to Christianity are very often provided with at least one "EGYPTIAN DOG STAR" or "TUAT STAR" which has since been relabeled "MOGEN DAVID" or "STAR OF DAVID" by European Jews. This is traditional of the fact that there are TWO PHASES of the Judaeo-Christian religious mystique. The first is JUDAISM; the second CHRISTIANITY. Yes, the people who made all of this possible were no different from those shown on pages 96 - 97 following. They equally appear on other pages throughout this volume. But the JEWS at the top of page 96 ancestors , not having   been unfortunate enough to have amalgamated with Europeans in Europe and   European-America to become "WHITE SEMITES, " are now being segregated RACIALLY and RELIGIOUSLY far beyond the extent of those shown at the bottom of page 96 and on page 97.

On pages 67 through 79 the intricate details on the CROSSES and CRUCIFIXES are of no higher quality in craftsmanship than that in the accompanying paintings. Yet the ELONGATED [facial characteristics and body] STYLE displayed in so many of the ETHIOPIAN PERSONAGES within the paintings and crosses, etc. is typical of the AFRICAN ART SCHEME which never reached European artists. This goes back all the way to PHARAOH AKHENATEN [Amenhotep IVth] in ca. 1370 - 1352 B.C.E. - during the XVIIIth Dynasty, as I have detailed in my book - BLACK MAN OF THE NILE AND HIS FAMILY, Chapter I, pages 1 - 72, etc., a few exhibits of which I have extracted and shown on many pages of this volume   along with other samples of fellow Africans from other parts of AFRICA [Alkebu-lan] on page 32. Here too you will note that the HUMAN HEAD or HOUSE OF THE BRAIN, according to African teachings, was more often than not purposely made to appear larger and disproportionate to the rest of the HUMAN BODY. Why? Because traditionally Africans have always considered the HUMAN HEAD to be...

"THE CENTER OF UNIVERSAL KNOWLEDGE"....[1]

Please remember that in this same context there is no such MASK and/or STATUE as a "FETISH" unless it was created and made in the City of "FETE, " Ghana [formerly called "Gold Coast Crown Colony, Ashante, Northern Territories," etc.]. Let us hope that the "THICK LIPS, BROAD NOSE, ELONGATED VESTIGAL BREASTS, " etc., etc.,

---

1. This typical practice is still prevalent in many West African art style. In Egypt it was most prevalent during the reign of Pharaoh Akhenaten.

etc. which supposedly caused "PHARAOH AKHENATEN" to become "MENTALLY ILL" and "PHYSICALLY DEFORMED" according to the so-called "modern" [WHITE RACIST] "scholars" of "WHITE ACADEMIA" will not happen to all of us who have the same so-called "PHYSICALLY DEFORMED" condition or "DISEASE". Other examples of the commonality of African ART, CULTURE, PEOPLE, LANGUAGE , RELIGION , etc. are equally obvious in the previous comparative samples just like those in professor Cheik Anta Diop, THE AFRICAN ORIGIN OF CIVILIZATION: MYTH OR REALITY? [ed. and transl. by Prof. Mercer Cook, New York, 1973]; see pages 67 - 79 and compare.

Just as we have been witnessing these intricately comprehensive exhibits of the commonality of the AFRICAN HIGH-CULTURES from the most ancient antiquity before the creation and manhood of Adam and Eve in the Garden of Eden sometime before the Christian Era [according to the Five Books Of Moses] [1] up to the present latter half of the Twentieth Century C.E., just so it must be asumed that we have been able to di-surn the need for further AFRICAN [Black] AUTHORS of every discipline to once again write AFRICAN PEOPLE's historical heritage in everything we have done to date; thus another aspect of our BLACK THEOLOGY.

On pages 10 - 24 we have seen pictures of many ancient structures of Ta-Merry [Egypt], Ta-Nehisi [Sudan] and Meröe [part of Sudan] the indigenous Africans from as far SOUTH as the Empire of Monomotapa like the following King and Emperor on page 94 engaged in PLANNING, DESIGNING, ENGINEERING and BUILDING to their own...

"ONE AND ONLY TRUE GOD" [name to be added],

all of which European and European-American writers of every kind attributed to only one group of Africans they called "THE EGYPTIANS" for reasons we have already examined in many of my works. But was it not ITIOPI [Ethiopia] and PUANIT the "EGYPTIANS" wrote in their MOST SACRED SCRIPTURES that everyone of their own

"GODS CAME FROM" and "LOVE TO BE IN THEIR NETHERWORLD"?

The importance of African lands SOUTH of "EGYPT" even made countless pharaohs and queens travel for numerous visits to their "ROYAL FAMILY" and "SHRINES TO THE GODS." The most noted of these journeys was that of Queen-Pharaoh Hatshepsut sometime during her reign over Egypt in ca. 1515 - 1484 B.C.E., a description of which I have shown on page 284 from an extract in her own Temple at "THE VALLEY OF THE PHARAOHS "in my book - BLACK MAN OF THE NILE AND HIS FAMILY, etc.

Certainly this entire work - from the Title Page to page 97 of this Chapter -

1. See Y. ben Jochanan's A CHRONOLOGY OF THE BIBLE; challenge to the standard
   version for chronological presentation of the creation of the so called "Holy Bible",
   etc.

93

"WHITE THEOLOGY" PREACHED BY THOUSANDS OF WHITE "MISSION-
ARIES" SAID THAT HE WAS AN "UNCIVILIZED HEATHEN." DO YOU TOO?

LE GRAND ROY ... MONO MOTAPA

*[Partial English translation]

"The Great King, Monomotapa. Very powerful and rich in
gold. Several kings are tributary to him. His territory comprises
Lower Ethiopia....His empire is very large and has a cicuit of
2,400 miles. His court is at Zimboae. There are women in his
guard...He has a great number of them in his army which give
great help to the men. He also has a great number of elephants.
His subjects are black, brave and swift runners, and he has
very fast horses. Idolators, sorcerers, and thieves are severely
punished."

"APARTHEID" IS EQUALLY PART OF "WHITE THEOLOGY" AS
MUCH AS "WHITE KLU KLUX KLANISM" IN WHITE RACIST
SOUTH AFRICA [Monomotapa]; AND WHERE ELSE YOU KNOW?

brings to our attention the obvious BIGOTRY
of ETHNOCENTRICISM and RACISM inherent in all RELIGIONS and their
"CHOSEN PEOPLE". This most of
us will certainly deny. WHY? Because we have nothing else but con-
tinuously NEGATIVE reactions to
"RACE" and "RELIGION" in our own
African-European, African-American
and African-Caribbean experiences in
the so-called "DIASPORA". The previous example on page 74, like those
on pages 73 and 82, etc. should be as
convincing as our belief in our "HOLY
SCRIPTURES"; at least more so, for...
"SEEING IS BELIEVING".... Thus, do we
need any more proof for our justification
of a "BLACK THEOLOGY" that is pre-
dicated on a "BLACK GOD" who "MADE"
and/or "CREADTED MAN IN HIS OWN"
[BLACK] "IMAGE"?

   I CERTAINLY DO NOT.

LOCHMAN or LOQMAN, whom the
Greeks called "AESOP," from a print in
the Bibliotheque Nationale, Paris (France
"Caucasoid", according to European-
American educators of ethnology, etc.!

Did his "BLACK THEOLOGY" affect the
"WHITE THEOLOGY" presently being
taught by the Jesuit Priests of the Roman
Catholic Church, Ku-Klux-Klan, Protestant Ministers, Jehovah Witnesses, Mor-
mons, et al to Black/African People in
Africa, the U.S.A. and the Caribbeans?

Louis Molina, "great" Catholic reformer
(Bibliotheque Nationale, Paris)
A SPANIARD

At prayer. Members of the choir, wearing prayer shawls, await signal. Other"Negro"Jewish communities are set up in Philadelphia, Brooklyn, Pittsburgh, Chicago and Youngstown, Ohio.

Alphabet lessons. Children of the Commandment Keepers Congregation are taught Hebrew.

Hebrew is official language of Israel and youngsters learn language at school. Here dark-skinned Jewish youth gets instruction in writing on the blackboard.

OTHER THAN A "WHITE RACIST SEMITIC THEOLOGY" TAUGHT BY WHITE RABBIS IN EUROPE, EUROPEAN-AMERICA AND ISRAEL; WHAT MAKES THE ONLY WHITE PERSON ON THIS PAGE THE ONLY "TRUE JEW," ETC. ?
A WHITE THEOLOGY BY WHITE AUTHORITY.
WHAT WILL CHANGE IT? A "BLACK THEOLOGY" BY BLACK ISRAELITES.

MOSES MARRIED THE "DAUGHTER OF THE HIGH PRIEST OF ETHIOPIA."
WHY SHOULD HER 20th CENTURY C.E. RELATIVES HAVE TO PROVE
THEIR "JEWISHNESS" AND NOT THEIR FELLOW "JEWS" FROM RUSSIA?
WHITE [Semitic] RACISM IN JUDAISM!

THE NEW YORK TIMES, FRIDAY, MARCH 4, 1955.

Falasha Jews From Ethiopia Studying in Israel

Their Tribe Practices Judaism According to Law of Moses

By HARRY GILROY
Special to The New York Times.

KFAR BATYA, Israel, Feb. 25 —Twelve young Falasha Jews, who might be taken as living proof of the legend that today's Ethiopians descend from Solomon and the Queen of Sheba, are studying at this children's village.

They come from a tribe, numbering 50,000, scattered over Ethiopia. The tribe is called Falasha, which in the Amharic tongue means "stranger." Its members practice Judaism according to the law of Moses, but have no tradition about later feasts such as Hanukkah and Purim.

The youngsters are here for two years of training. They are in a beautiful farm school adjoining Raanana on the Sharon plain—established and operated by the Women's Mizrachi Organization of America. Hadassah, the American Women Zionists, is aiding the project through Youth Aliyah, to which it contributes.

There are ten boys and two girls in the Falasha group. The other children of Kfar Batya have made them welcome.

Bible Read in Amharic

Details about the Falasha were supplied by the director of Kfar Batya. He is a stocky young man named Leonard Rauchwerger, a native of Vienna who had to flee medical school there because of Hitler. He subsequently was drafted while at the City College of New York and wounded in Italy, and then as a G. I. student at the Hebrew University of Jerusalem ran into the Arab-Israeli war.

Mr. Rauchwerger sent a Falasha lad for the oldest boy and girl. The boy came first, a tall 16-year-old who gave his name as Isazah Adomic. He said he had learned English from a military school in Addis Ababa.

The girl was 15. She said her name was Malka (Hebrew for Queen) Avraham. Mr. Rauchwerger said she was translating from her native name of Negus, which is the royal title. .

Isazah said they had read the Bible in a dialect of the Amharic tongue. It was the custom of his people, he said, for all the men and women of the tribe to gather for prayers. Some of the tribe were priests.

The older pair were soon joined by several younger boys and also by a ring of curious but friendly white boys. The Falasha said they liked what they had seen of Israel—the farm work, food and soccer games at Kfar Batya and that Hebrew was a hard language. One wrote rapidly in Amharic. It was translated —

they were having a good time and liked their companions.

The Falasha tribe practiced the ancient rite of animal sacrifice up to twenty years ago, according to Zvi Weiss of the Youth Aliyah Department of the Jewish Agency for Palestine. He said that the Falasha contend they are descendants of Israelites who went to Ethiopia when Sheba returned from her stay with Solomon. The Queen, according to their legend, had a son Menelik by Solomon.

There are other theories about the origin of the Falasha. One is that they were Ethiopian converts to Judaism at some ancient time. Another is that they are the descendants of a Hebrew mercenary army that fled southward along the Nile when their

Egyptian employer was overthrown. A third idea is that they emigrated from the Arabian peninsula, either in Biblical times or after the rise of Islam.

Reports of Jewish tribes in Africa have been noted by historians and travelers many times in the last thousand years. But the Falasha themselves apparently did not know that Judaism still existed outside Ethiopia.

Prof. Joseph Halevy of France visited the Falasha in the Eighteen Sixties. In 1904 Dr. Jacob Faitlovitch, Professor Halevy's pupil, went to visit them and thereafter devoted his life to bringing them back into the world communion of Judaism. His work resulted in the coming of Falasha students to Israel and in the development of Hebrew education in Ethiopia.

Isazah Adomic, 16-year-old leader of Falasha youngsters studying at Kfar Batya in Israel, serves Malka Avraham. Another Falasha student and an Israeli friend await their turns.

For details on the above Yosef ben-Jochannan's WE THE BLACK JEWS: WITNESS TO THE "WHITE JEWISH RACE" MYTH [unpublish manuscript being prepared for publication by Alkebu-lan Books Associates]. Do not be misled into believing that the one or two White Jewish organizations conducting their Christian-type missionary work on the so-called "Falashas" are so doing because of altruistic reasons. All of them are insisting that they/we accept European and European-American type WHITE RACIST TALMUDIC JUDAISM in place of TORAHDIC JUDAISM. For example: students are being trained to dislike "POLYGAMY" the same as imposed on the Yemenite Jews, etc.

BIBLIOGRAPHY

[Books, Magazines, Newspapers, unpublished manuscripts, etc.]
All of the listings are not necessarily according to alphabetical
order; they are mostly listed according to usage in the preparation
of the manuscript. It is suggested that the works that I have not
cited specifically be read as added documentation to the text herein.
Books cited in the main text might be repeated in this bibliography.

WORKS ON THE HISTORY AND GOSPEL OF JESUS "THE CHRIST":

Koiñe Bible [original New Testament written between ca. 50 - 100 C.E. or A.D.]

M. S. Enslin, The Prophet from Nazareth, New York, 1961

B. H. Streeter, The Four Gospels, London, 1924

G. Higgins, Anacalypsis, London, 1840 [2 Vols.]

"The Rise Of Christianity" [in Cambridge Ancient History, Vol. XI, 1936]

A. Schweitzer, The Quest Of The Historical Jesus, London, 1910

J. Klausner, Jesus of Nazareth, London, 1929

A. Cleage, Jr, The Black Messiah, New York, 1970

M. Smith, Clement of Alexandria and a Secret Gospel of Mark, Cambridge, 1973

C. Guignebert, Jesus, London, 1935

St. Augustine, On Christian Doctrine, Numidia, ca. 430 C.E. [any English translation]

A. T. Olmstead, Jesus, in the Light of History, New York, 1942

J. M. Robinson, A New Quest for the Historical Jesus, London, 1959

S. G. F. Brandon, Jesus and the Zealots, New York/Manchester, 1967/68

M. R. James, The Apocryphal New Testament, Oxford, 1926

A.D. Doyle, "Pilate's Career and the Date of the Crucifixion" [in Journal of Theological Studies, Vol. XLII, Oxford, 1941]

S. G. F. Brandon, The Trial of Jesus of Nazareth, London/New York, 1968

P. L. Maier, "Sejanus, Pilate, and the Date of the Crucifixion" [in Church History - U.S.A, Vol. XXXVII, 1968]

P. Winter, The Third Trial of Jesus, Berlin, 1961

Sir J. Frazer, The Golden Bough, London, 1928 [13 Vols.]

A. N. Sherwin-White, Roman Society and Roman Law in the New Testament, Oxford, 1963

S. Zeitin, Who Crucified Jesus?, New York, 1942

Josepheus Flavius, Jewish Antiquities, Books XIV - XV

E. Schurer, Geschichte des jusdischen Volkes im Zeitalter Jesu Christi, Band I [3 -4 Aufl., Leipzig, 1901, translated into English as "The Jewish People in the time of Jesus," Edinburgh, 1890]

Rachid's Aquarian Gospel [n. d.; another portion of the BOOKS removed from the Bible]

S. Perowne, The Life and Times of Herod the Great, London, 1956

E. M. Smallwood, "High Priests and Politics in Roman Palestine" [in Journal of Theological Studies, Vol. XIII, Oxford, 1962]

W. R. Farmer, Maccabees, Zelotes and Josephus, New York, 1956

R. Eisler, The Messiah Jesus and John the Baptist, London, 1931

J. W. Jack, The Historic Christ, London, 1933

J. Hastings [ed], Encyclopaedia of Religion and Ethics, 1914 [8 Vols.]

Y. Yadin, Masada: Herod's Fortress and the Zealots' Last Stand, London, 1966

R. Bultmann, Primitive Christianity in Its Contemporary Setting, London, 1960

W. O. E. Oesterley, Immortality and the Unseen World, London, 1930

C. H. Dodd, The Bible and the Greeks, London, 1954

R. M. Grant, Gnosticism and Early Christianity, London, 1959

G. G. M. James, Stolen Legacy, New York, 1954

J. Doresee, The Secret Books of the Egyptian Gnostics, London, 1959

J. Baillie, The Belief in Progress, Oxford, 1950

E. Dinkler, The Idea of History in the Ancient Near East, New Haven, 1955

M. Werner, The Formation of Christian Dogma, London, 1957

P. de Labriolle, History and Literature of Latin Christianity, London, 1924

WORKS ON PHARAOH AKHENATEN:

G. Massey, Egypt the Light of the World, New York, 1928 [2 Vols.]

------ , The Book of the Beginnings, New York, 1927

C. Alfred, Akhenaten: Pharaoh of Egypt - a new study, London, 1968

A. H. Gardiner, Egypt of the Pharaohs, Oxford, 1961

A. Weigall, The Life and Times of Akhenaten, London, 1922

G. Maspero., History of Egypt, London, 1888 [13 Vols.]

------- , The Dawn of Civilization, London, 1900 [8 Vols.]

J. A. Wilson, The Culture of Ancient Egypt, Chicago, 1960

Sir E. A. Wallis Budge, Gods of the Egyptians, London,

M. Murray, Akhenaten, New York, 1967

J. H. Breastead, The Dawn of Conscience, New York, 1934

-------- , Ancient Records of Egypt, New York, 1936

Y. ben-Jochannan, BLACK MAN OF THE NILE AND HIS FAMILY, New York, 1972

W. M. Flanders Petrie, Tell-el-Amarna, London, 1889

T. E. Peet and L. Woolley, The City of Akhenaten, Oxford, 1922 [Vol. I]

H. Frankfort and J. D. S. Pendlebury, The City of Akhenaten, Oxford, 1933 [Vol. II]

J. H. Breasted, Ancient Records of Egypt,

J. H. Wilson, The Burden of Egypt, Chicago, 1952

W. M. Flinders Petrie, Tell - el - Amarna, London, 1889

T. E. Peet and L. Woolley, The City of Akhenaten, Oxford, 1922 [Vol. I]

H. Frankfort and J.D.S. Pendelbury, The City of Akhenaten, Oxford, 1933 [Vol. II]

W. Stevenson-Smith, The Art and Architecture of Ancient Egypt, Baltimore, 1958

S.A.B. Mercer, The Tell - el - Amarna Tablets, Toronto, 1939

E.F. Campbell Jr., The Chronology of the Amarna Letters, Baltimore, 1964

H. Frankfort [ed], The Mural of el Amarnah, London, 1929

C.E. Wilbour, Travels in Egypt, Brooklyn, 1936

Davies and Gardiner, The Tomb of Huy, London, 1926

H. Carter, The Tomb of Tut Ankh Amen, London, 1923/33

A. H. Sayce, Hittite Letters on Egypt, London, 1922

E. Billie-DeMot, The Age of Akhenaten, New York/Toronto, 1966

L. Cottrell, Life Under the Pharaohs, New York/Chicago/San Francisco, 1960

J. Baikie, Egyptian Antiquities in the Nile Valley, London, 1932

I.E.S. Edwards, The Pyramids of Egypt, New York, 1952

A. Erman, Blackman and Aylword, The Literature of the Ancient Egyptian,
    London, 1927

A. Erman, A Handbook of Egyptian Religion, London, 1907

------, Life in Ancient Egypt, New York, 1927

Sir A. Gardiner, The Attitude of Ancient Egyptians to Death and the Dead, Cam-
    bridge, 1935

S.R.K. Glanville, The Legacy of Egypt, New York/Oxford, 1942

Dr. M. Murray, The Splendour That Was Egypt, New York, 1949

A. Weigall, The Glory of the Pharaohs, New York, 1923

W.M.F. Petrie, The Building of a Pyramid in Ancient Egypt, London, 1930

T. Davis, G. Maspero, et al, The Tomb of Queen Tiyi, London, 1910

W.C. Hayes, The Scepter of Egypt, Part II, New York, 1959

J. Cerny, Ancient Egyptian Religion, London, 1952

Sir E.A.Wallis Budge [transl.], The Egyptian Book Of The Dead and Papyrus Of Ani,
    London, 1895 [2 Vols.]

Y. ben-Jochannan, Black Man Of The Nile, New York, 1969

WORKS ON OSIRIS or HORUS: THE FIRST "CHRIST":

Sir E. A. Wallis Budge, The Egyptian Book of the Dead and the Papyrus of Ani, London, 1895 and 1913 [2 Vols.]

S. A. B. Mercer, The Pyramid Texts, New York, 1952 [4 Vols., transl. into English]

------ , The Pyramid of Unas, New York, 1968 [4 Vols., transl. into English]

A de Buck, The Egyptian Coffin Texts, Chicago, 1935/56 [8 Vols., Transl. into English]

T. G. Allen, The Egyptian Book of the Dead, Chicago, 1960 [transl. into English]

L. G. Griffiths, The Origins of Osiris, Berlin, 1966

Sir E. A. Wallis Budge, Osiris and the Egyptian Resurrection, London, 1911 [2 Vols.]

H. W. Smith, Man and His Gods, Boston, 1961

A. Bye, Osiris or Horus: The First Christ in History, London, 1918

Sir E. A. Wallis Budge, Osiris, London, 1898

E. Otto, Egyptian Art and the Cults of Osiris and Amon, London, 1968

H. Frankfort, Kingship and the Gods, Chicago, 1948

L. Spence, Myths and Legends of Ancient Egypt, London/Sydney, 1922

R. E. Witt, Isis in the Graeco-Roman World, Ithaca, New York, 1971

A. Alföldi, A Testament of Isis in Rome, Budapest, 1937

H. I. Bell, Cults and Creeds in Greco-Roman Egypt, Liverpool, 1953

T. A. Brady, The Reception of the Egyptian Cults by the Greeks, New York, 1935

E. A. W. Budge, Legends of the Gods, London, 1912

-----, From Fetish to God in Ancient Egypt, London, 1932

R. T. R. Clark, Myth and Symbol in Ancient Egypt, London, 1959

J. T. Dennis, The Burden of Isis: being the laments of Isis and Nephthys, London, 1910

J. G. Griffiths, The Conflict of Horus and Seth, Liverpool, 1960

E. Lversen, The Myth of Egypt and its Hieroglyphs in European Tradition, Copenhagen, 1961

A. S. Peake, A Commentary on the Bible, London, 1919

R. E. Witt, The Egyptian Cults in Macedonia, Balkan Studies, Thessalonica, 1970

--- , The Flight into Egypt, Studia Patristica XI, Berlin, 1971

A. Churchward, Signs and Symbols of Primordial Man, London, 1920

----------, Origin and Development of Religion, London, 1928

----------, Arcana of Freemasonry, London, 1929

Y. ben-Jochannan, The Black Man's Religion and Extracts And Comments From The Holy Black Bible, New York, 1973

WORKS ON MOSES AND HIS FIVE BOOKS:

A. Eban, My People: The Story of the Jews, New York, 1968

M. Fishberg, The Jews, London, 1911

R. Graves and R. Patai, Hebrew Myths: The Book Of Genesis, New York, 1964

A. Hertzberg [ed.], Judaism, New York, 1962

A. R. Johnson, The Cultic Prophet In Ancient Israel, New York, 1940

T. J. Meek, Hebrew Origins, New York, 1960

Osterly and Robinson, History of Israel, New York, 1934

R. S. Smith, Religion of the Semites, New York, 1935

S. A. Cook, The Religion of Ancient Palestine in the Light of Archaeology, New York, 1930

L. Finklelstein, The Jews: Their History, Culture and Religion, New York, 1949 [3 Vols.]

M. Herskervitz, Are The Jews A Race?, London, ?

J. W. Jack, The Date of the Exodus, New York, 1925

T. Doane, Bible Myths and their Parralels, New York, 1910 [2 Vols.]

S. Mendelssohn, The Jews of Africa, Especially in the Sixteenth and Seventeenth Century, New York, 1920

T. E. Peet, Egypt and the Old Testament, New York, 1922

     ---, Teachings of Amen - em - eope, New York, 1922

J. J. Williams, Hebrewism in West Africa..., etc., London, 1931

A. Wakigorski, The Jews in Africa, Cairo, 1966

FIVE BOOKS OF MOSES [Pentateuch or Holy Torah]

WORKS ON THE LIFE OF MOHAMET AND TEACHINGS ABOUT AL'LAH:

Dr. E. W. Blyden, Christianity, Islam and the Negro Race, New York, 1905

M. Balfwil, The Life of Mohamet, [n. d.]

J. C. de Graft-Johnson, African Glory, London, 1954

P. K. Hitti, Makers of Arab History, New York, 1940

----, History of the Arabs, London, 1927

Sir W. Muir, Life of Mohamet, London, 1894

A. Sabe, Al Koran, 1784

A. A. Syed, Life and Teachings of Mohammed, London, 1891

A. Tor, Mohammed: The Man and His Faith, 1936

J. H. Kramers, The Legacy of Islam, New York, 1931

H. A. MacMichael, A History of the Arabs of the Sudan, New York, 1922

R. Warren, Mohammed, Prophet of Sudan, New York, 1965

ADDED WORKS FOR EXTRA DOCUMENTATION:
[Some of these may have been listed previously]

Al-Jahiz   THE MERIT OF THE TURKS.
--------   THE SUPERIORITY OF SPEECH TO SILENCE.
--------   THE PRAISE OF MERCHANTS AND DISPRAISE OF OFFICIALS
--------   THE SUPERIORITY IN THE GLORY OF THE BLACK RACE OVER
                THE WHITE, CAIRO, EGYPT, 1906.
--------   THE BOOK OF ELOQUENCE AND RHETORIC.
--------   THE BOOK OF ANIMALS, Vol's. I - VII.
Ashe, G.   GHANDI New York, 1968.
Apuleius   THE GOLDEN ASS.
Allen, W.F.; Ware, Charles P. and Lucey, M. Garrison (eds.) SLAVE
                SONGS OF THE UNITED STATES, New York, 1867.
Aptheker, H.   AMERICAN SLAVE REVOLTS, New York, 1943.
Arnold, Sir T. W.   THE PREACHING OF ISLAM, London, 1913.
Achebe, Chinua.   THINGS FALL APART, New York, 1959.

Brooks, C.H.   A HISTORY AND MANUAL OF THE BRAND UNITED ORDER
                ODD FELLOWS IN AMERICA, Philadelphia, 1893.
Biobaku, S.   RELIGION IN CONTEMPORARY AFRICAN LITERATURE,
                New York, c1966.
Burnet, J. (ed.)   THE WORKS OF PLATO (In: Oxford Classical
                Texts, 5 vols. 3rd ed., New York, 1888).

Cicero.   DE OFFICIIS.
Churchward, Dr. A.   ORIGIN AND EVOLUTION OF FREEMASONRY, London,
                1920.
----------   ARCANA OF FREEMASONRY, New York , 1915.
----------   ORIGIN AND EVOLUTION OF THE HUMAN RACE,
                London, 1921.
Collingwood, R.G.   ROMAN BRITAIN, Oxford , 1932.
Clavier, A.   BIOGRAPHIE UNIVERSELLE, Vol. VIII, PARIS, 1844.
Cronon, E.D.   BLACK MOSES, Madison, Milwakee, London, 1968.
Coppin, L. J.   UNWRITTEN HISTORY, Philadelphia, 1920.

Darwin, Sir Charles.   THE NEXT MILLION YEARS, London, 1952.
Denon, Baron.V.   TRAVELS IN UPPER AND LOWER EGYPT, London, 1789.
Dumond. D. W.   ANTISLAVERY. The University. Ann Arbor. Michigan,
Danquah, Dr. J.B.   AKAN LAWS AND CUSTOMS, London, 1928.
-------   THE AKAN DOCTRINE OF GOD, London. 1944.
Diodorus   SICULUS, Book XVII (n.d.).
Digby, Sir Keneln.   POWER OF SYMPATHY, London, 1660.
Davidson,   THE AFRICAN SLAVE TRADE, New York, 1968.
--------   THE AFRICAN PAST, New York, 1964.
--------   AFRICAN KINGDOM, New York, 1968.
deLas Casas, Bishop Bartolome.   HISTORIA de las INDIAS, Madrid,
                1519.

el-Yezdi, Haji Abu.   THE KASIDAD (as translated by Sir Richard
                F. Burton), London, 1878.
Erskine, Mrs. Stewart.   THE VANISHED CITIES OF NORTHERN AFRICA,
                London, 1927.
Emperor Galerius.   IMPERIAL EDICT OF MAY c305-311 A.D.
Eddy, Mrs. Mary Baker   SCIENCE AND HEALTH WITH A KEY TO THE
                SCRIPTURES, (1876).
----   MANUAL OF THE MOTHER CHURCH. (1888).
Erdman, J.E.   A HISTORY OF PHILOSOPHY, Vol. I., 1910.
Eusebius   ECCLESIA TICAL HISTORY. TII.
Esiun-Odom   BLACK NATIONALISM, Boston, 1961.
Faucet, A.H.   BLACK GODS OF THE METROPOLIS.
Fisher, M.M.   NEGRO SLAVE SONGS IN THE UNITED STATES, Ithaca,
                New York, 1959.

Franklin. J.H.   FROM SLAVERY TO FREEDOM, New York, 1964.

Frobenius, Leo   AFRICA SPEAKS, 3 Vols., London, 1913 (latest
                  edition, 1969).
Fickling, S.M.   SLAVE CONVERSION IN SOUTH CAROLINA: 1830-1860
                  (Univ. of S.C., 1924).

Geddes, Michael   CHURCH HISTORY OF ETHIOPIA, 1969.
Gaton-Thompson, G.   THE ZIMBABWE CULTURE, 1931.
Garrucci, R.   LA MONETE DELL'ITALIA ANTICA. Parte Secunda,
                  LXXV, Roma, 1885.
Garrucci, R.   LA MONETE DEL' HALIA ANTICA, Parte Secunda,
                  LXXV, Roma, 1885.
Gibbs, H.A.R.   ARAB LITERATURE, London, 1926.
Gibbon, N.   DECLINE AND FALL OF THE ROMAN EMPIRE, Vol. I,
                  Vol. IV, Dublin. 1781.
Gaunt, Mary   WHERE THE TWAIN SHALL MEET, London, 1922.

Higgins, Sir Geoffrey.   THE CELTIC DRUIDS, London, 1892.
Huart. C.   LITERATURE ARABE. Pari 1902.
Herodotus   HISTORIES, Book II (as translated by Aubrey
                  Selencourt), New York, 1954.

Higgins, Sir Geoffrey   ANACALYPSIS, Vols. I-II, London, 1840.
Harmack   MISSION AND EXPANDSION, Vols. I-IV.
Helibdorus   ETHIOPIAN HISTORY UNDERDOWNE, 1857 (London, 1895).
Hook. S.H. (ed.) MYTH AND RITUAL, 1933.
Hinde, Capt. S.L.   THE FALL OF THE CONGO ARABS, 1897.
Hertslet, Sir E.   THE MAP OF AFRICA BY TREATY, 3 Vols, London,
                  1903.
Hughes   SATIRE OF THE SOCIAL PROBLEM OF THE NEGRO IN
                  AMERICA. (n.d.).

Jack, J.W.   THE DATE OF THE EXODUS, 1925.
Johnson, Rev. S.   THE HISTORY OF THE YORUBAS, 1937.
Jackson, F.J. Foakes, and Lake, K.   THE BEGINNING OF CHRISTIANI-
                  TY, 1933.
Johnson, J.W. and Johnson, R.   BOOKS OF AMERICAN NEGRO SPIRITUALS.
                  New York, 1940
Jernegan, M.W.   "Slavery and Conversion in the American
                  Colonies" (In: THE AMERICAN HISTORICAL
                  REVIEW, Vol. XXI, April. 1961)
Jaeger, Werner   ARISTOTLE:FUNDAMENTALS OF THE HISTORY OF HIS
                  DEVELOPMENT, O.U.P., 1932.

Lincoln, C.E. BLACK MUSLIMS, Boston, 1961.
Liebevitch, L.   ANCIENT EGYPT, Cairo, Egypt, 1958.
Leslau, Wolf FALASHA ANTHOLOGY, New Haven, 1951.
Langer, W. L. (ed.)   ENCYCLOPEDIA OF WORLD HISTORY, New York,
                  1952.
Lull, Raymond LULL REPORTS (Haklyut Society, London).
Labourete, H. AFRICA BEFORE THE WHITE MAN, Boston, 1963.
Liciado LIFE OF BARTOLOME DE LAS CASAS, Madrid, 1565.
Lewis and Schacht (eds.)   ENCYCLOPEDIA OF ISLAM.

Mendelsohn, Jack   GOD, ALLAH AND JUJU. New York, 1962.
Northcott. W.C.   CHRISTIANITY IN AFRICA, Philadelphia. 1963.
Massey, G.A.   BOOK OF THE BEGINNINGS, vol. II, London.
Mays, B.E. and Joseph W. Nicholson. THE NEGRO CHURCH. New York.
Moon, Parker T.   IMPERIALISM AND WORLD POLITICS, New York, 1934.

Nesfield. J.C.   BRIEF VIEW OF THE CAST SYSTEM, India. 1885.

106

Nevinson, Henry   A MODERN SLAVERY, New York, 1906.

Oates, W.J.   BASIC WRITINGS OF ST. AUGUSTINE, New York, 1948,
              2 Vols.
Ortiz, Fernando   LA AFRICANA DE LA MUSICA FOLKLORICA DE CUBA,
                  La Habana, 1950.

Parrinder, Geoffrey   AFRICAN MYTHOLOGY, London, 1967.
Polski, C. and Brown, R., Jr. (eds.)   THE NEGRO ALMANAC, New
                                        York, 1967.
Plutarch   ALEXANDER "THE GREAT" (n.d.).
Palgrave, C.   ESSAYS ON THE EASTERN QUESTION, London, 1967.
Parker, R.A.   THE INCREDIBLE MESSIAH, Boston. 1937.

Rogers, Joel A.   SEX AND RACE, Vol. I, New York, 1945.
------   WORLD'S GREAT MEN OF COLOR, Vol. I, New York,
        1954.
------   NATURE KNOWS NO COLOR LINE, New York, 1950.
Robertson, A.   ORIGINS OF CHRISTIANITY, New York, 1962.
Ratzel, F.   HISTORY OF MANKIND, Vols. I-II, London, 1869.

Sithole, Nda baningi   "An African Christian View" (In: CHRIST-
                       IANITY IN THE NON-WESTERN WORLD, ed.
                       by C.W. Forman, Englewood Cliffs,
                       New Jersey, 1967).

St. Augustine   ON THE BEAUTIFUL AND THE FIT (c370-373 C.E.).
------------   CONFESSIONS.
------------   ON CHRISTIAN DOCTRINES.
------------   HOLY CITY OF GOD.
------------   DRAMATIC POEMS (c377 C.E.).
------------   AGAINST THE ACADEMICS, ON THE HISTORY OF LIFE.
------------   ON ORDER.
------------   DE VITA BEATA.
------------   ON MUSIC.
------------   ON THE MORALS OF THE CATHOLIC CHURCH AND OF THE
               MANICHEANS.
------------   RETRACTIONS.
------------   DE ORDINE.
St. Cyprian   THE LAPSED.
----------   THE UNITY OF THE CATHOLIC CHURCH.
Stanley, H.M.   DARKEST AFRICA, New York, 1890.
Snow, C.P.   (Comments in JOHN O'LONDON'S WEEKLY, London, 1952)
Solomon, King   THE PROVERBS (c976-936 B.C.E.).
Smith, Prof. Elliot   HUMAN HISTORY, London, 1934.
Suyuti, S.   HISTORY OF THE CALYPHS (translated by H.S. Jar-
             rett, Calcutta, 1881).
Sabine, G.H.   A HISTORY OF POLITICAL THEORY, New York, 1961.
Schofield, J.N.   HISTORICAL BACKGROUND OF THE BIBLE, London,
                  New York. 1938.
Stewart. J.A.   THE MYTHS OF PLATO, U.O.P., 1905.
Slade, R.   BELGIAN CONGO, Oxford, 1962.
Sonnerson, S.   RAPE OF AFRICA.
Stace, W.T.   A CRITICAL HISTORY OF GREEK PHILOSOPHY, New York,
              1920.

Tanner, B.J.   AN APOLOGY FOR AFRICAN METHODISM, Baltimore,
               1867
Talbon. P.A.   NIGERIAN FERTILITY CULTS, London, 1927
Tertullian   DE ANIMA.
----------   THE TREATISE AGAINST HERMOGENES

Volney, Count C.C.   RUINS OF EMPIRES, London, 1890

Zeller, E.   A HISTORY OF PHILOSOPHY FROM THE EARLIEST PERIOD
             OF TIME TO SOCRATES (translated by S.F. Alleyne)
             2 Vols.,London. 1881.

Wells, H.G.   A SHORT HISTORY OF THE WORLD, New York, 1956.
Wildernissen, D.   STANLEY IN AFRICA, Vols. I-II, Germany, 1887.
Weidner, Dr. D.   A HISTORY OF AFRICA SOUTH OF THE SAHARA (etc.),
                   New York. 1968.
Wesley, C.H.   THE LIFE EXPERIENCE AND GOSPEL LABOURS OF RT.
                   REV. RICHARD ALLEN, Philadelphia (n.d.).

Young, C.   POLITICS IN THE CONGO, Princeton, N.J., 1965.

Religious Books and Documents

        APOSTLES' CREED.
        BABYLONIA TALMUD (6th Century C.E. version).
        *COFFIN TEXT (religious history of Egypt).
        *HOLY BIBLE (Septigiant, Vulgate, Rhames Duoy,
                and Kings James versions).
        *HOLY KORAN (Qu'ran - Moslems' or Muslims' Bible).
        *HOLY TORAH (Five Books of Moses - Hebrews or
                Jews Bible).
        *HYMN OF ADORATION (from Egyptian Coffin Texts).
        NEGATIVE CONFESSIONS (from Egyptian Coffin Texts).
        THE TEACHINGS OF AMEN-EM-OPE (original source of
                "Solomon's Proverbs" - c1405-1370 B.C.E.).
        THE PROVERBS OF KING SOLOMON (Texts from Hebrew Torah
                or Bible - c976-936 B.C.E.).
        THE EXORDIUM (Texts from Muslim or Moslem Koran).

*Note: The names or titles- Holy Koran, Holy Bible, Holy Torah
and Holy Talmud are outgrowths of the Sacred Coffin Texts, Pyramid Texts and Teachings of Amen-em-ope, etc.

Periodicals, Documents, Paintings

C. P. Snow's Comments in JOHN O'LONDON'S WEEKLY, (London, 1952).
CHRIST AND BARABBAS (A Painting by Verlat in the ROYAL MUSEUM OF
                ANTWERP, Belgium).

EDWIN C. SMITH PAPYRUS (A composium of medical writings from
                Egypt, BROOKLYN MUSEUM, Brooklyn, New York,
                N.Y.).
EBERS PAPYRUS (Most ancient "Birth Control Recipe" known to man-
                kind, Egypt, c1550 B.C.E., LONDON MUSEUM, London).
ENCLYCLICAL OF POPE JOHN XXII.
ENCYCLICAL OF POPE CLEMENT VIII (Giulino de Medici).

HARLEM'S RELIGIOUS BIGOTS (F. Rasky's article in TOMORROW, Vol.
                9, November, 1949).
MAP OF AFRICA (See: Black Man of the Nile, by Y. ben-Jochannan,
                New York, 1970, p. 252).
MANIFESTO OF THE NATIONAL BLACK ECONOMIC CONFERENCE (Detroit, Mich.,
                April 26, 1969)

108

PROTEST CHURCHES DIVIDED ON THEIR URBAN CRISIS PROGRAMS (New York
          Times, Sunday, May 18, 1969)

THE MESSENGER (Official organ of the Nation of Islam, a weekly
          Newspaper).
THE DAY (Father Divine's Peace Mission News Weekly and Official
          Religious Organ).
THE NEGRO ENIGMAN (Article by Prof. M.D.W. Jeffreys in: WEST
          AFRICAN REVIEW, September, 1951).
TEL-EL-AMARNA (14th Century B.C.E. Egyptian-African Dispatches).
THE UNIVERSAL ETHIOPIAN ANTHEM (From a poem by Burrell and Ford:
          "Ethiopia, Thou Land of Our Fathers ").

UNIVERSAL DECLARATION OF HUMAN RIGHTS (United Nations Organization,
          New York, N.Y., 1949).
UNITED STATES OF AMERICA CENSUS REPORT (from 1920 to 1970 C.E.).

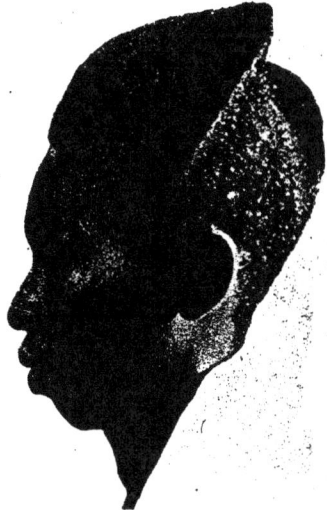

WHICH ONE IS THE "SEMITE" OR THE "NEGRO"? [Left] PHARAOH RAMESES II.
[Right] A 20th CENTURY C.E. TUSI [see Denise Cappart's article "Reflet du Monde,"
1956, and Cheikh Anta Diop's The African Origin Of Civilization: Myth Or Reality?,
ed. and transl. by Mercer Cook, New York, 1973, page 19, plate 11]

Note: The bibliographies in all of my other works can be also used as supplimentary
documentation for this volume.

Photo by Tumani, "State of the race Conference",
Los Angeles, California, October 1977 C.E./A.D

Greetings in the spirit of Pan-Africanism as
represented by a "Black/African Theology!

Additional works available by Dr. Ben

A Chronology of the Bible: Challenge to the standard version.
Yosef ben-Jochannan.1972*,1995. 24 pp.(paper $4.00, ISBN
0-933121-28-8). Chronology documents the African origins of
Judaism, Christianity, and Islam. Dr. Ben traces some of the
significant influences, developments, and people that have shaped
and provided the foundation for the holy books used in these
religions.

African Origins of the Major Western Religions. 1970*, 1991.
363 pp. (paper $24.95, ISBN 0933121-29-6). First published in 1970,
this work continues to be instructive and fresh. Dr. Ben critically
examines the history, beliefs, and myths that are the foundation of
Judaism, Christianity, and Islam. He highlights the often overlooked
African influences and roots of these religions. The Black Classic
Press edition is a facsimile edition, with an added index and extended
bibliography.

Black Man of the Nile. 1972*, 1989. 381 pp. illus. bibl. (paper
$24.95, ISBN 0933121-26-1). In a masterful and unique manner, Dr.
Ben uses *Black Man of the Nile* to challenge and expose
"Europeanized" African history.   He reveals distortion after
distortion made in the long record of African contributions to world
civilization. Once these distortions are exposed, he attacks them with
a vengeance, and provides a spellbinding corrective lesson. Of all the
works published by Dr. Ben, this one remains a treasured all-time
favorite. Readers continue to demand this work.

Abu Simbel to Ghizeh. 1987*, 1989. 350 pp. illus. gloss. (paper
$22.00, ISBN 0933121-27-X). This tour guide is an alternative to
guides written for and by Europeans. Dr. Ben draws from his many
years of travel, study, and living in Egypt to provide a useful history
and guide to ancient Egyptian/African monuments, cultural sites, and

prominent people. Although it is intended for readers who plan to travel to Egypt, this guide is helpful to anyone who wants to gain a better understanding of ancient African history.

Africa: Mother of Western Civilization. 1971*, 1988. 750 pp. illus. bibl. (paper $34.95, ISBN 0933121-25-3). Dr. Ben examines the African foundations of Western civilization. In lecture essay format, he identifies and corrects myths about the inferiority and primitiveness of the indigenous African peoples and their descendants. He mentions many authorities on Africa and their works and proves how they are racist in intent. Dr. Ben is often humorous, and always critical of traditional Western scholarship and values.

We The Black Jews. 1983*, 1993. 408 pp. (paper $24.95, ISBN 0933121-40-7). Dr. Ben destroys the myth of a "white Jewish race" and the bigotry that has denied the existence of an African Jewish culture. He establishes the legitimacy of contemporary Black Jewish culture in Africa and the diaspora, and predates its origin before ancient Nile Valley civilizations. This work provides insight and historical relevance to the current discussion of Jewish and Black cultural relationships.

To order, send a check or money order to:
Black Classic Press
P.O. Box 13414
Baltimore, MD 21203-3414
Includes $3.00 for shipping the first book and $2.00
for each additional book ordered.
Credit Card Orders Call—1-800-476-8870
Please have your credit card available.

* *indicates first year published*

www.ingramcontent.com/pod-product-compliance
Lightning Source LLC
LaVergne TN
LVHW021451080426
835509LV00018B/2238